the Children's Media Yearbook 2023

The Children's Media
FOUNDATION

The Children's Media Yearbook is a publication of The Children's Media Foundation

Director, Greg Childs

Administrator, Jacqui Wells

The Children's Media Foundation

15 Briarbank Rd

London

W13 0HH

info@thechildrensmediafoundation.org

First published 2023

Cover and book design by Rebekkah Hughes

ISBN 978-1-9161353-5-2

The Children's Media
FOUNDATION

Contents

Editors' Foreword

Hannie Kirkham, Research and Strategy Manager, Oriel Square and **Dr Ashley Woodfall**, Senior Principal Academic, Bournemouth University

Adopting a longstanding tradition from children's comics like *The Beano* or *Whizzer and Chips* (for those with longer memories!), we are very happy to introduce this 'Bumper Edition'. At 152 pages, 40 articles and 60 contributors, it's our fullest one yet, and we like to think it offers both useful insight and some timely and vital debate.

Children's media feels like it is at a critical juncture: we are living through a revolution in the ways that children and young people interact with content. Online and social media are far more popular with children than any other platform, including television. In this evolving landscape many children no longer engage with media that we might recognise as being 'public service' (either explicitly or implicitly) or that has been made specifically *for* UK children – and this framing inflects almost all other debate on children's media.

The *Yearbook* features articles written by people who create media for children, who are engaged in policy and advocacy work and who are actively researching the field (be they conducting market or scholarly and scientific research). For example, in this year's edition (alongside a number of articles that demonstrate the significance and positive influence that media can have in a child's early years) we share persuasive research on how rhyme – coupled with repetition and reading out loud – are key to children's language development. Although incorporating rhyme might pose a challenge regarding international saleability, this year we also showcase some success stories in this area.

Beyond the expected discussion on what are challenging policy and funding conditions within the UK, we also consider children's media from a 'smaller nations' perspective – looking at the landscape in Wales, Northern Ireland and Scotland, as well as in Denmark and Norway: there is much to celebrate here, but equally some lessons and warnings. Other areas of *Yearbook* discussion include the representation of fatherhood in children's media, an area where the industry has perhaps long fallen short. And talking of falling short, we also address the ways in which women are welcomed (or not) back into our production community post maternity, and we look at ways to build authenticity into content, products and teams.

There is plenty of other 'good stuff' across the *Yearbook* – with rich discussion on gaming, children's media facing wellbeing, writing for preschool, directing kids, and so much more!

We can't offer you a free cover gift or pull-out poster, but we do hope you enjoy this 'boredom busting' bumper edition.

Sleepwalking Into The Future:
Time For Radical Solutions?

Anna Home OBE, Chair, The Children's Media Foundation and **Greg Childs OBE**, Director, The Children's Media Foundation

For the Children's Media Foundation (CMF), this year has been dominated by our increasing concern over the long-term future of public service media (PSM) for children and young people. This follows the abrupt closure of the Young Audiences Content (YAC) Fund in early 2022 and is in the context of the slow progress through parliament of the Online Safety Bill and changes to the regulation of content for children proposed in the draft Media Bill.

The evaluation of the YAC Fund in the spring highlighted how successful it was in increasing the range of PSM content across different age ranges and fulfilling a clear public service remit with stringent criteria – benefiting both the audience and the industry. However, there is little chance of a new fund appearing anytime soon. Meetings with government ministers have made it clear that while there is enthusiasm for what the Fund achieved, there is simply no public money to pay for a replacement. Cuts at the BBC and their re-prioritising children's budgets to focus more on animation and internationally viable content, and a clear warning from the commercial public service broadcasters that life without the YAC Fund was going to mean less commissioning, means the range of content will certainly diminish.

ITV has since replaced the CITV channel with an on-demand service on ITVX – with even lower budgets – and both Channel 5 and Channel 4, while they committed to try to maintain some of the new programming commissioned with the YAC Fund, could not promise to increase their commitment when they met industry representatives at an All Party Parliamentary Group (APPG) meeting convened by CMF and chaired by Baroness Benjamin OM DBE.

More recently Alex Mahon, Channel 4's Chief Executive, has reiterated their commitment to young people and raised the issue of the adverse impact of AI-driven algorithms on platforms heavily watched by the young. This makes the government decision not to privatise Channel 4 at least one positive in this rather bleak landscape.

The whole ethos of children's media is changing at speed. The traditional children's TV audience is fragmenting. Viewers are migrating to a variety of different providers; in particular TikTok and YouTube, neither of which will be sufficiently regulated by the Online Safety Bill to ensure prominence for public service content on their platforms. Without intervention, children will become less and less aware of what public service media is, and of where and how to find content that not only entertains them, but reflects them, their needs, concerns and interests, and helps them to develop as citizens of the future.

Over the last year CMF has been addressing these issues and promoting discussion of this bleak future in a variety of ways.

We have allied with a number of charities in the Children's Coalition, led by Baroness Beeban Kidron's 5Rights organisation, which has sponsored a series of amendments to the Online Safety Bill, ensuring it enshrines the concept of 'safety by design'. And we work with another coalition of organisations, convened by the Voice of the Listener and Viewer, which is currently planning responses to the Draft Media Bill that will reflect growing concern over the future of public service media in the UK.

CMF is particularly concerned about what appears to be a proposed relaxation of regulation. Currently the proposals need clarification. But they appear to state that instead of each individual broadcaster being assessed annually for their children's or youth output – the regulatory stance defined by the 'Benjamin amendment' in the 2017 Digital Economy Act – in future we may return to the situation in which Ofcom is only required to assess the vague concept of 'sufficient content' across all the broadcasters' outputs 'taken together'. This is the failure of regulation that led to the dramatic decrease in commissioning defined by Ofcom as 'market failure'. Baroness Benjamin has worked with CMF on a letter that has been sent to the Secretary of State at the Department for Culture, Media and Sport (DCMS) requesting clarification of the intentions in the draft Bill. Longer term the prominence and discoverability of children's PSM content is a serious issue – for the industry, for the audience and for society at large.

No-one is effectively addressing the 'lost audience' of aged 7+ children for whom public service content will soon not even be a memory. Former Director of Children's at the BBC Joe Godwin has written an important contribution to this debate in this *Yearbook*. It stresses the need for government, the regulator and broadcasters to address children where they *are*, rather than where they think they should be.

CMF has been stimulating the debate through the course of the year – as part of our role to ensure the issues are brought to the attention of the industry, the public and politicians. Our public events have discussed what happens after the YAC Fund and, most recently, *Sleepwalking over the Edge* considered why public service content for children and young people is vital not only for their futures but for the future of society as a whole. "Sleepwalking" was a term used by BBC Director of Children's and Education Patricia Hidalgo at her address to the APPG in March. At CMF we are determined to wake up the people with the power to change this. Our next steps are to brief politicians of all parties about the long-term implications of a failure to act now and the inadequacy of the Media Bill to address the problem of the lost audience.

Image by dooder on Freepik

We are also pursuing research partnerships to address the question of whether or not investment in PSM can impact positively on young people's development, and how it can be delivered effectively in the new landscape. If you have research expertise to offer please contact us, and to keep up with the issues discussed in this article – and throughout the *Yearbook* – you can subscribe to the CMF newsletter, come to our events, become a supporter or patron. If you want to get more actively involved, please message: director@thchildrensmediafoundation.org

This year at CMC the Foundation is producing the Question Time session at the start and the debate, *Public Service – RIP*, at the end. We hope these will both shed further light on the critical issues facing the children's media industry and the young audience.

Radical solutions will be required. We need to find a way to secure the future for the long term. Propping up the past is not enough. But if we all pull together to make our voices heard, perhaps by this time next year we could be looking at a more optimistic future.

THE CHILDREN'S MEDIA CONFERENCE

4–5–6 JULY 2023

POWER UP!

The Children's Media Conference is the annual gathering of professionals engaged in communicating to and entertaining kids and young people in the UK, Ireland and beyond.

CMC is a proud supporter of the Children's Media Foundation and pleased to be able to distribute the Children's Media Yearbook to all our CMC 2023 delegates.

Follow, join and chat to us at:

- @childmediaconf
- the children's media conference
- the children's media conference
- childmediaconf
- contact@thechildrensmediaconference.com
- www.thechildrensmediaconference.com

100 Years Of Disney

Dr Amy M. Davis, Lecture in Film Studies, University of Hull

When I was 5 years old, way back in the mid-to-late 1970s, my grandmother took me on my first ever trip to Walt Disney World. That was a while ago, of course, so my memory of it consists mainly of mental snapshots backed up by a few photos. There were rides, photos with characters, and *lots* of treats. In one photo, I'm standing in front of Cinderella's castle holding a rapidly-melting ice cream sandwich, thus combining snacks and making photographic memories. In short, it's glorious to visit Disney World aged 5 with your grandmother but *not* your parents or little brother, and I definitely recommend it. I got to be queen for a day at the Magic Kingdom, but it was more than that: it was the day I fell in love with Disney World, and when my interest in all things Disney was first well and truly piqued.

Naturally, that trip wasn't my first-ever encounter with Disney, even if I was a member of what Professor Kay Stone referred to in 1975 as the 'post-Disney generation'.[1] I had Disney books and toys, and I was an avid viewer of both new and re-run Disney television shows. Ironically, my 'come to Disney moment' coincided with the era when its executives habitually asked themselves "What would Walt Do?" It was a challenging time, and the deaths of its founders (Walt in 1966, Roy in 1971), as well as changes to Hollywood and America, had knocked Disney's confidence, killing its willingness to take risks and transforming it from an entertainment industry leader to a follower. When Kay Stone called those born between 1960 and 1975 'post-Disney', it was to this she was referring: a company that had been great, once upon a time, but its king and crown prince had died and it had lost its way.

Photo: courtesy of Dr Amy. M Davies

But how had it got there? And how did things get better?

---

[1] Kay Stone, "Things Walt Disney Never Told Us," from *The Journal of American Folklore*, Vol. 88, No. 347, Women and Folklore (Jan.-Mar. 1975): 42-50; Quote from p. 49.

When, in October 1923, Walt Disney persuaded his brother, Roy, to run the business side of his new studio (a smart move, since Walt had declared bankruptcy just five months earlier at the ripe old age of twenty-one), they founded – officially on 16 October 1923 – the Disney Brothers Studio. It was tiny, but within months they had graduated to a storefront on Kingswell Avenue in Hollywood, though they still had to film live-action sequences in empty lots and alleyways as their studio had room only for the bare necessities of animation production. Their first series, the silent *Alice Comedies*, featuring child actress Virginia Davis (no relation) as well as assorted animated characters, did well. But in 1927, Disney and their distributor, Winkler Productions, decided to retire it and move to full animation with *Oswald the Lucky Rabbit*. By then, Walt Disney Productions (as it was renamed in January 1926) had moved on to bigger, posher premises, a whole building of their own on Hyperion Avenue. It was here, in early 1928, that the brothers learned that most of their staff – apart from Walt's long-time friend Ub Iwerks and a handful of others – would be leaving, taking *Oswald* with them. A clause in their contract with Winkler Productions meant Disney had never owned the rights to *Oswald*; it was a hard-learned lesson to be careful to retain – and protect – their copyrights going forward, resulting in Disney becoming notoriously litigious. It was also out of this mess that Mickey and Minnie Mouse were born.

Though not *everything* they attempted was successful, between 1928 and 1949, the small independent Disney studio took some great risks and had some incredible successes. In 1928, *Steamboat Willie* was the second 100% sound film to be released, and the first to get sound right (especially in its use of music). In 1932, Disney released the first film made with 3-Strip Technicolor, securing a three-year exclusivity contract with Technicolor that meant Disney would be the only studio using the technology until 1935. In addition to the debuts of many beloved shorts and iconic characters, it's also the period when Disney made and released *Snow White and the Seven Dwarfs* (1937). Indeed, *Snow White* was so revolutionary that it has wrongly been remembered as the first *ever* animated feature film. Do note, British readers: when it was released in the UK in 1938, the BBFC slapped an A certificate on it; if you wanted to see *Snow White* in the UK and were under 18, you had to bring an adult with you. Yes, the decision was controversial; it also shows how avant garde the film was.

But the year after *Snow White*, World War II began in Europe. For Disney, now located on the Burbank campus where its headquarters are located today (built using profits from *Snow White*), this meant a period of increasing financial struggle: first, through losing revenue from European distribution, and then when (beginning in January 1942) it began making information and training films commissioned by the US government and military, often at a loss for Disney. There was even a contingent of the army stationed at the studio, who maintained a 24-hour guard and anti-aircraft guns to protect the Lockheed plant nearby. The 1940s were so difficult that it wasn't until 1950 that Disney could afford to release a single-narrative animated feature. But that film, *Cinderella* (1950), saved the studio's finances and launched the first true Disney renaissance: a number of classic animated films, its first live action features, and its move into television. Two wildly successful Christmas-day specials in 1950 and 1951 were produced and, on 27 October 1954, their first series, *Disneyland*, debuted on ABC (the network Disney would buy in 1996). *Disneyland* helped raise money for – and synergistically advertised – the theme park being built in Anaheim. Disneyland's opening day was broadcast live as a special episode of *Disneyland* on 17 July 1955.

Believe it or not, the early reviews of Disneyland the park declared it a failure, not least because the park was still unfinished on opening day. But Walt's response to these critics was that Disneyland would never be finished; it would always be a work in progress. That has proved true, as new attractions, shops and restaurants have opened, older venues closed, and the park continues to evolve. Critics in 1955 may not have been impressed, but the general public – including many there on opening day – loved it. Less than two months later, on 8 September 1955, Disneyland had its 1 millionth guest (fittingly, her name was Elsa – 4 year old Elsa Marquez, who was crowned a Disney princess for the day). It would welcome its 100 millionth guest on 17 June 1971, four months before the opening of Walt Disney World in Florida in October 1971.

Of course, during the time between the openings of Disneyland and Disney World, a lot would change. In some ways, things continued to grow. WED Enterprises (now Walt Disney Imagineering), founded in 1952 to help design Disneyland, would continue to innovate for the Disney parks, which became for years the main source of revenue for the Walt Disney Company (by the early 1980s, the parks provided roughly 80% of Disney's earnings). The live-action film

division, however, was fairing less well by the 1970s. As animator Don Hahn noted in his 2009 documentary *Waking Sleeping Beauty*, "Around that time [1981], the studio did a survey that revealed a majority of teenage moviegoers wouldn't be caught dead near a Disney movie." Arguably, Disney hit its lowest point in 1984 when, to survive a hostile takeover attempt, it paid out $328 million in greenmail. But even when things were difficult, innovations continued. EPCOT theme park opened on 1 October 1982 as part of Disney World's expansion. The Disney Channel launched on 18 April 1983. It would go on to spin off other channels as cable television expanded. Likewise, the founding of Touchstone Pictures in 1984 would expand Disney's perceived demographic. The late 1980s saw the beginning of the second Disney renaissance as they re-invested in their animation division. Though things would slow for a time in the late 1990s, by the late 2000s Disney had returned to form and began a period of major expansion and acquisition, culminating in its purchase of 21st Century Fox in March 2019. In the UK (from 2015) and the Philippines (from 2018), Disney began DisneyLife, a streaming service that likely served as a test run for its eventual launching of Disney+ on 12 November 2019 in North America and the Netherlands. Its major international rollout began just in time for the Covid-19 pandemic's first lockdowns, a coincidence that likely contributed to its reaching its five-year goal of 100 million subscribers in only 16 months. Even with some recent setbacks, it is still arguably the biggest streaming service worldwide.

Disney has weathered many storms in its one-hundred years, from the Great Depression and World War II to the Covid-19 pandemic (which saw its resorts closed for months and then limited re-openings for months after). Most recently, it is dealing with attacks on the company – and especially on Walt Disney World – by Florida's governor for taking a stance against his openly anti-LGBTQ+ legislation. There are those saying that Disney's lawsuit against the governor, announced 26 April 2023, may well have far-reaching implications as regards First Amendment protections (Disney is arguing that it is being punished for speaking out against the governor's homophobic legislation, a clear First Amendment violation); its outcome, of course, remains to be seen. But for now, the Disney company – publicly, at least – is most focused on the celebration of its 100th anniversary, one it has reached often against great odds, to come out at the top of the Hollywood pecking order.

As for *why* it has succeeded for a century… naturally, that is up for discussion. I would argue that, from the beginning, Walt and his team recognised the power of storytelling. Their primary medium was film, but music, merchandising, and theme parks were soon utilized alongside cinema. As for the stories they told, Disney long ago found a way to turn anything into a fairy tale, and to make fairy tales feel contemporary. Furthermore, Disney has always seen their target audience in the broadest terms. As Walt Disney (supposedly) once said, "… in planning a new picture, we don't think of grown-ups, and we don't think of children, but just of that fine, clean, unspoiled spot down deep in every one of us that maybe the world has made us forget and that maybe our pictures can help recall." By not talking down to children, and at the same time allowing adults the freedom to re-embrace their inner child, Disney ensured life-long fandom. Ultimately, Disney's success is explained by their combining ancient storytelling themes with modern storytelling technologies. After 100 years, it's proved itself a winning formula.

Not bad for a corporation that started in a garage rented for a few dollars a month by two enterprising brothers, one of whom had a very, very big dream.

Raven: The CBBC Gameshow – Twenty-One Years On

Colin Ward, Producer and Co-creator of *Raven*

In the late autumn of 2001, I had just finished producing *Jungle Run* for CITV – my first ever gameshow – and I was looking for a new project. *Jungle Run* was originally commissioned by Nigel Pickard, who had then left CITV to become Controller of the restructured BBC Children's Department. The BBC was getting ready to launch its new digital children's channels and Nigel had commissioned a gameshow from BBC Scotland to debut on CBBC. But he wanted to be sure they found the right Producer to work on the project.

The revamped series of *Jungle Run* I produced for CITV had done well, getting strong audience figures and a BAFTA nomination, so I got a call from BBC Scotland and headed north to create a show that, 21 years later, gets fantastic, positive responses from people who still have fond memories of James Mackenzie announcing, "Let the challenge begin!" *Raven* became an iconic show for the children's audience and that passion continued for 20 years, with repeats of the original ten series and, in 2017, a reboot that introduced Aisha Toussain in the role of Raven.

But as is often the case, when we were dreaming up the games and writing scripts we had absolutely no idea it would be so successful. *Jungle Run* had been a big, high-profile show on a main broadcast channel and CITV had given it an unusually large budget of around £60k per episode for a 20-episode run. The shows on the BBC's new digital channels were given much lower budgets. From memory, I think the first series of *Raven* had about £28k per episode for a 20-episode run.

I was given a lot of freedom to develop the format for the show. Nigel Pickard was keen on two aspects of the original pitch: he insisted the audience should see the lochs, mountains and forests of Scotland, and the gameplay had to involve the gradual elimination of contestants until the winner was revealed. (The pilot show for the pitch had been called *Decimator* and although it had elimination in the gameplay, there was a very different overall game structure. It was also set in a contemporary story world; I seem to recall there was a quad bike challenge, which would never have worked in *Raven*!) Outside of those two requirements, we had the freedom to reimagine the concept and, for the most part, the Execs left us to our own devices. At the time, I remember thinking that *Raven* was being made to help fill the CBBC schedule, which needed a lot of new content. We were working on a low-budget gameshow and no one was really expecting us to make anything award-winning.

That's not to say I didn't have to fight a few battles to get what I wanted. The first disagreement came over the production design team. I was asked to work with a BBC production designer, but I was adamant we had to bring in the people I had worked with on *Jungle Run*; Tom Barker and Liz Barron. Tom and Liz were fantastic designers and prop-makers who knew how to stretch a tight budget. They also had experience working on shows like *Crystal Maze*, so they knew how to design games.

In the end, BBC Scotland agreed and nearly all of the original *Raven* games were created by the three of us working together. But I had definitely upset a few people. Understandably, I was seen as an outsider who had been brought up from England and was now taking away jobs that should have gone to Scottish talent. In that first year I must have been a real pain in the neck for some of the people working at BBC Scotland. But over the four years I spent there, I was fortunate to work with so many amazing, talented people, like our Production Manager, Jilly Welsh, who had a passion for children's programming and was totally committed to the show.

Series 1 of *Raven* went into production around Easter 2002 and I was there through to the final dubs, which must have been in September or October. And I can tell you the whole show was directly inspired by *The Lord of Rings*. They released *The Fellowship of the Ring* into cinemas in December 2001 and, for me, a lifetime wish had been granted. Like many young boys, I had read and re-read Tolkien's fantasy adventure and I was desperate to see that world brought to life. Peter Jackson's films gave me that and my love of the stories was reawakened. So when I was taken to look at Castle Howard – our fantastic filming location 'across the water' on the Cowal peninsular – all I could see was Strider leading a group of young hobbits through the woods. I wanted the character of Raven to be our Strider. He would train the young warriors by setting them a series of challenges, hoping to find the Ultimate Warrior. And you can see the influence of Tolkien in the tone of the script, the map graphics and many of those early games, such as The Riddle Bridge and The Old Troll.

The challenges and the overall structure of the gameplay were worked out in pre-production by Liz, Tom and me. For the overall structure, we just adapted computer gaming tropes into a live action gameshow; six warriors, each with seven lives represented by feathers on their standard. If a warrior failed a challenge they lost one of their lives and a feather from the standard. Lose all your lives and it was game over.

On location for The Riddle Bridge

Courtesy of Colin Ward

In the challenges there were opportunities to win gold rings—thank you *Sonic*—and the warrior with the fewest number of rings at the end of the day would face elimination. They would get one last chance; they had to overcome the final challenge, which was called the Way of the Warrior. That game was devised by Liz and Tom and they produced drawings for an amazing, wooden obstacle course about 40 metres long, with moving shields and swinging axes that could knock you off the path. Now remember, this was a low-budget show, but they managed to recruit a talented team of local craftspeople to work with them and made deals with suppliers to create a fantastic climax to the show. At the wrap party, we all took it in turns to have a go, with mixed results that bore absolutely no relation whatsoever to the relative quantities of alcohol consumed.

On location for The Way of the Warrior

Tom and Liz's work set the standard for the show. I recall the Senior Camera Operator telling me that when they were assigned to work on *Raven* they thought it was just going to be a low-budget kids' show. But when they came on the recce and saw what Tom and Liz had built for the Way of the Warrior, it changed how everyone felt about the project. There was an almost conscious decision to go the extra mile for the show. Anyone who worked at the BBC back in the day will recall it was very helpful to have your department heads onside, because they could pull in a few favours to get the equipment the show needed and couldn't really afford. We definitely could not afford a production truck, but we managed to get a land rover rigged up with some racking, a receiver and three monitors. The landy had room for me, the Director and our inestimable and scarily efficient PA/Researcher, Samantha Lockhart. From there we could at least watch what we were shooting, although there was no 'live' talkback with our three camera operators so we had to rely on two-way radios.

When a warrior lost a life, we wanted it to look the same as in a computer game, with the character vanishing from the action and then 'respawning' in a different location. This turned out to be a good move. I still remember sitting in the edit suite waiting for the lightning bolt visual effect to 'render' and then playing back the sequence for the first time. We listened to the tense music building up as the young warrior approached the fatal moment and watched as the lightning bolt came shooting down from the sky to obliterate him from the face of the earth. My editor stopped the playback and there was a brief moment of stunned silence. I turned to him and asked: "Did we just kill a kid?"

But it was that sense of there being something important at stake that gave *Raven* its audience appeal. I had one golden rule for the team: always take the challenges seriously and make sure the warriors face every challenge for real. My reasoning was that this would help the kids to take the adventure seriously as well. I wanted them to feel like they were doing something amazing. I wanted to see their desperation to do well in the performances, because this would enhance the drama and the impact of the story for the audience.

It worked. That first series of *Raven* was a runaway success for CBBC and over the next ten years the show played its part in establishing an identity for the channel. In the autumn, as we finished post-production, we sent off our VHS tape to BAFTA and fully expected to hear nothing more about it. The BBC had certain shows it wanted to push for awards and our little gameshow was definitely not on the list. But BAFTA had a jury system and, according to one of the members who spoke to me on the night, they saw something fresh and original in the show. So, to everyone's joy and surprise, that first series of *Raven* won the BAFTA for best Children's Entertainment Programme and it then won again in 2006 for Series 4.

As I said, when you are working on something new, you don't really know if it's going to be any good. I suppose that when we saw the audience figures and were awarded the BAFTA, we realised we had made a good show. But for me, my moment of real pride came later, when a colleague at the BBC told me how a teacher had asked her about this new BBC kids' show called *Raven*. She'd never seen it but she wanted to know why all her kids were going out into the playground with their coats worn as cloaks. And why were they setting each other tasks and shouting out, "Let the challenge begin"? Now *that* is a prize worth having.

There is a short postscript to this story. Many years later, when I had left the BBC and returned to Yorkshire, I came across an article in our local paper, the Bradford *Telegraph & Argus*. It was about a young woman who was running her own hair salon. The reason for the story was that she had struggled at school with attendance and discipline, but her life had turned around when a researcher from the BBC picked her to take part in a CBBC gameshow, even though her school was reluctant to even let her audition. The researcher was Samantha and the young woman was known to me as the warrior Brhea, who came third in that first series. She was a terrific competitor who tackled the challenges as though her life depended on it.

So that is just one example of a kids' TV series making a difference to someone's life. And yes, perhaps the fact we tried to put certain values at the heart of every *Raven* story – honesty, courage, determination, resilience – made no difference to the many hundreds of thousands of children who loved the show. And perhaps today's children's audience is still getting those values from the content they enjoy on YouTube and TikTok, which are now dominating children's media experiences. Let's hope so. Because it is highly unlikely anyone would make that level of investment in either *Jungle Run* or *Raven* today, at least not if the target audience was restricted to UK kids. And even if someone did commission them, would the audience even find the show? I am sure I am biassed, but it feels like 21-years ago was a 'golden age' for children's gameshows. As the quote goes, life is what happens when you are busy planning something else. I was lucky enough to be in the right place at the right time.

Remembering I'm (Still) A Womble:
70 Years Of Wombling

Mike Batt, singer-songwriter-producer of *The Wombles*

When I was 19, I was signed as an artist to Liberty/United Artists records and given the ridiculously exalted position of Head of A&R (signing and recording artists). I only stayed there for 18 months and then left to go freelance as an arranger/producer, while remaining signed as an artist. Having not had a hit by then as an artist, and in order to keep the wolf at bay, I wrote jingles. Rice Krispies, Guinness, Smarties, The Humphries for Unigate milk. One day in 1972 my jingle agent told me that there was a production company making something called "The Wombles" for the BBC and asked if I fancied a talk to them about the title music. I went along and met the brilliant animator-director Ivor Wood (*Magic Roundabout*, and later *Paddington* and *Postman Pat* among many) and was immediately fascinated by the characters he was animating. He explained their ethos – cleaning up Wimbledon Common – and their genesis – a walk on said Common by author and broadcaster Elisabeth Beresford and her two young children, Marcus and Kate. Kate had mis-pronounced "Wimbledon Common" as "Wombledon Common". This had given Liza (as we all called her) the idea to create *The Wombles*. She went immediately home and spent days at her typewriter knocking out a first draft, creating Great Uncle Bulgaria, Orinoco, Tobermory and all the others.

Liza's books had come out a couple of years earlier, and done moderately well. Well enough for the BBC to have become interested – yet the illustrations in the book had them looking just like teddy bears. Ivor had re-designed them with the familiar pointy noses and grey fur, and Bernard Cribbins had narrated and given them voices. I fell in love with the characters. I asked Ivor if he might prefer a song, so that viewers could identify with some of the characters and their activities before even seeing a single frame of the show. He liked the idea, and it wasn't long before I had written the now well-known "The Wombling Song" (sometimes referred to as "Underground, Overground").

Courtesy of Mike Batt

Wellington, drawn by Mike

In those days I used to chance the rent money by spending it on making records in the hope that I could sell my 'product' to a record company and get back to the landlord with the rent before I got kicked out of my flat. This was one such record, but I found it hard to sell to a willing label. Almost by fluke I eventually licensed it to CBS (now SONY) records because the Head of A&R's son liked it! But in order to have the record company take me seriously (!) I realised they needed a walking, talking version of a Womble who could sign autographs and attract attention. My mum had always been good at costume making, and obliged with the first ever costume, that of Orinoco. I walked into the record company and they were suddenly delighted and interested in promoting the record with me.

One day, the promotion man from the record company called me and asked me if there was an actual group of Wombles. I lied and said yes, which turned out to be the right answer because he said "That's great because the producer of *Top Of The Pops* has said he wants you on *this week* if you are a full group". This left me with a delightful problem. The TV show was the day after that. I only had one costume! My mum, dad, two brothers and our sister all convened and spent all night sewing and gluing three more costumes just in time, and I recruited three friends of mine to be the other band members. That was 'breakpoint' for us, because it wasn't long before the band had hit number four in the charts and the perception of the Wombles had transcended children's television and become a household name throughout the whole family. It's too long a story to tell you how we developed the band and built it up for so long, but we had eight hit singles and four gold albums, winning the Music week Magazine

award for the biggest-selling recording artists of 1974! The other singles were "Remember You're A Womble", "Banana Rock", "Wombling Merry Christmas", "Minuetto Allegretto", "Wombling White Tie And Tales", "The Womble Shuffle" and 'Let's Womble To The Party".

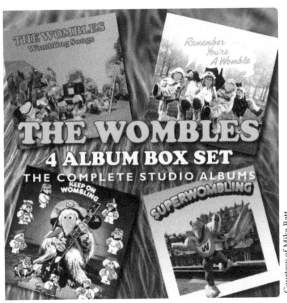

Courtesy of Mike Batt

Even though I did not own the underlying copyright of the characters, I had negotiated the music and pop group rights instead of taking a £200 fee for my theme song. So I wasn't involved in vast merchandising and TV programmes sales, books, etc. However, it was a really successful and fun two years, which, despite lumbering me with a rather jolly, perhaps lightweight reputation that prevented me from being taken seriously as a solo singer-songwriter in this country, was a fantastic and life-changing experience. It was only when I wrote "Bright Eyes" for Art Garfunkel (for the film *Watership Down*), which went to number one for six weeks, and other more 'credible' hit songs and film scores, that my career began to be seen as more than a furry flash in the pan! I always felt I had been put on earth to write film scores, and to an extent I still do. I'm passionate about my work as a composer, orchestrator and conductor as well as producing and writing for others like Steeleye Span, Hawkwind, Katie Melua and the London Symphony Orchestra.

The Wombles, meanwhile, remain regarded as national treasures. Elisabeth wrote more books, and there was a 'come-back' TV series in the nineties. In 2011 I dusted off the costumes and brought the band out for our first ever fully live performance at Glastonbury – an exhausting experience in more than 80 degrees of heat! We pulled a massive crowd; bigger, so the Glastonbury folks told me, than the act on the biggest (Pyramid) stage at that time.

I flirted with producing and directing a new TV show about 10 years ago but after establishing an animation company especially for the project and incurring huge expense (creating three 15 minute episodes that will now never be seen)

we had to call it a day. I also lost the rights to various people who were able to take advantage of the situation, and there have, since, been character design changes which I don't feel have been helpful. However, life goes on, and *The Wombles* seems to remain popular and loved. When people ask me if I regret being involved, I always answer that I would not exchange my life with them for a different life without them. They provided me and my family with such joy. Hopefully I've done enough other work in all the genres I enjoy, for people to have seen the other facets to what I do.

Meanwhile, the trail-blazing eco-warrior message lives on with them. Very much ahead of their time, Elisabeth's characters set the scene for a mindset in young children and older folks alike. I'm deeply grateful that they fell into my lap all those years ago, and proud that I could help to make them into the phenomenon that they have become.

The Wombles live at Glastonbury Festival

Twenty Years Of Magic Light Pictures

Marc Ollington, Marketing Director, Magic Light Pictures; **Michael Rose**, Joint CEO and Co-founder, Magic Light Pictures and **Martin Pope**, Joint CEO and Co-founder, Magic Light Pictures

Marc Ollington talks to co-founders Michael and Martin about their 20 year adventure filmmaking with Magic Light Pictures.

The filmmaking partnership of Magic Light Pictures' co-founders Martin Pope and Michael Rose has now lasted for 20 years. It's been an extraordinary two decades for them, during which they've built one of the most enduring British animation production companies, bringing Julia Donaldson and Axel Scheffler's beloved children's books to the screen, including *The Gruffalo*, *Stick Man*, *Zog* and most recently *The Smeds and the Smoods*. In doing so, they have illuminated Christmas day television for millions in the UK, and their work has travelled all over the world winning countless awards. Along the way they've produced both live action and animated feature films, an Oscar nominated adaptation of Roald Dahl's *Revolting Rhymes* and they recently launched their first preschool series *Pip & Posy*.

They became friends in the early 1990s when Martin was producing his first feature film and Michael was a programme buyer at Channel 4. While Martin continued running his own successful business making feature films and TV dramas, Michael joined Aardman in Bristol as Head of Development before becoming joint producer of the third Wallace and Gromit short film *A Close Shave*. He went on to set up Aardman's feature film arm, executive producing *Chicken Run* and *Wallace and Gromit: Curse of the Wererabbit*. Meanwhile Martin's films included the BIFA and Evening Standard award-winning *Lawless Heart* and the Sundance hit *Touch of Pink*.

In 2002, Michael moved back to London and saw Martin's film *The Heart of Me*, which was the Closing Gala Film of the London Film Festival. The two got back together over coffee and realized the possibilities of working together.

Martin says, "I'd been running a company for years on my own, making films, telling stories, exploring great characters – and they'd done well, but it wasn't enough. I'd always wanted to find a partner so that together we could create a business which had real legs – and here was my old friend who shared that ambition."

"We talked a lot about what we wanted to do," says Michael. "We realized that we had very different skill-sets and experiences, but by joining forces we could build something really special. We were sufficiently different that we'd complement each other."

> "We shared the belief that what matters is not the technique you use, whether animation, live action or any kind of hybrid, but the stories you tell and the passion they're told with."

What comes across is a comfortable blend of business-focused pragmatism, with an enduring, overriding love for the stories and values of the actual work they make.

Martin remembers "standing on Wardour Street when we came up with three ideas which formed the bedrock of our business plan: make live action films first, develop animation, and if we could find the right property, build that into a lasting brand. So even at the beginning and even though we didn't know our exact next steps (or even sometimes where the rent was coming from) we already had the idea of a trajectory and where we wanted to go."

Michael agrees: "We knew that if we could develop an animation IP for the whole family, then it could have lasting worth, positively impact people over time, and could underpin our business."

Michael has fond memories of those early days, but it clearly wasn't an easy ride. "I do remember many scary moments and things were often tight. In the early years we dubbed third party animated films into English and produced a couple of live action feature films including *Sparkle*, starring Bob Hoskins, Lesley Manville and Stockard Channing, which Martin had developed as a follow up film with the wonderful directors of *Lawless Heart*. We also started a seven year journey to bring animated feature *Chico & Rita* to screen."

The Gruffalo-shaped lightbulb moment hit them early on when they discovered they were both reading the same book to their respective children at bed-time, *The Gruffalo*. As Martin says, "I remember when Michael first came in and said 'Have you been reading this? It's amazing.' And he was right. It was a delight for us as parents to read and it clearly delighted our children."

Michael takes up the story. "We were sure it was the 'one' and that we could create a classic

The Gruffalo

Pip & Posy

special but inevitably it took a long time to get the rights, four years in all from 2003 to 2007. *The Gruffalo* was already a huge publishing success and we had to convince Julia Donaldson, Axel Scheffler and publisher Macmillan that we were the best partner to bring it to screen."

I ask Martin about pitching for the rights to *The Gruffalo*.

"Many companies wanted it, some as a series, others as a feature film, but we wanted to stay true to the book and determined that it was perfect as a half hour Christmas special. There are various moments where I can remember Michael saying confidently, 'we're going to produce it for BBC One on Christmas day' and my heart was pounding, thinking, how on earth are we going to pull that off?!"

Martin continues, "that notion of creating a company with value – long-term value, rather than short-term productions – was the key change for me. Michael had been part of developing that with *Wallace & Gromit* at Aardman, but it wasn't his company; we were both now at the stage where we wanted to control our own destiny. Control has always been important for us, in many different ways."

Michael adds: "If you make a feature film, it can be wonderful. But by the time it's finished, you've lost control to the financiers. And profits are hard to come by. When it came to *The Gruffalo* we set out to create a very different model – we raised money privately so that we could control all stages of the journey from development through production to marketing, distribution and licensing so we could have the best chance of creating a classic children's brand. We wanted to ensure that we always delivered the highest quality to the audience at every touchpoint."

The enormous success of *The Gruffalo* in 2009, followed by *The Gruffalo's Child*, has since unfolded into a string of smash hit half-hour animations screened on BBC One and across the world. Through the decade these would become a Christmas staple for millions of us. Magic Light Pictures has given us a new British festive tradition, as we settle down on Christmas afternoon, stuffed full of food, to be transported by a beautiful, often thought-provoking, animated special.

Those films also launched a hugely successful Gruffalo brand. Perhaps it is this balance of production and brand building that enables Magic Light to thrive. Michael says: "We've built

Courtesy of Magic Light Pictures

The Smeds and the Smoods

Courtesy of Magic Light Pictures

Zog

a business that is known for wonderful films, some of which are enduring classics, viewed again and again, which we're pleased to think deliver an incredible pleasure to our family audiences. But alongside that, we've built a company with wonderful values at its root and those values cascade through all our work. We want to ensure that *The Gruffalo* is still a much loved classic brand in 50 years' time. If we err on the side of caution, it's because we need to get it right. In everything we do we're pushing for high quality with strong values which can have a long life."

Interjects Martin, "For instance our most recent film *The Smeds and the Smoods* turned out beautifully and I'm so proud of it. I think the values of it and the storytelling and animation encapsulate what we're aiming for. At the same time we're so delighted that *Pip & Posy* got into its second season so soon. It's a fantastic tribute to the team's work on that show. So as we look to the future we're proud of things we've done, and keen to do more, with more series and specials in our plans – but we're also always aware that everything we do is about the audience and delighting them so that huge challenge keeps us grounded."

Martin is proud of what Magic Light has achieved but his eyes light up when he talks about their growing team. "What I love is that there's so much variety and creativity, with people coming up with new, interesting and exciting work across the board, from development to apps to trails or different ways to reach and please our audience."

"Even just this weekend, I was looking at my local cinema, thinking, what shall I go and see? And there is *The Gruffalo* and *Zog* playing as a double-bill, Saturday and Sunday. How nice is that?"

Approaching **Doctor Who's 60th Anniversary**: The Doctor Will See You Now

Dr Matt Hills, Professor of Fandom Studies, University of Huddersfield

As it approaches its 60th anniversary on November 23rd 2023, *Doctor Who* (BBC, 1963–1989, 1996, 2005–) seems in relatively rude health. The BBC have entered into a deal with Disney which will see the show hosted on Disney+ outside the UK; the extremely popular actor David Tennant, who previously played the tenth Doctor, is about to return to the role for a series of three specials; and Bad Wolf have taken up the reins as the show's producers, reuniting a production team – including Russell T. Davies – who had previously worked on the show for BBC Wales. As if this weren't enough, Ncuti Gatwa and Millie Gibson have been cast as a new Doctor and 'companion' to star in yet another new era of the programme, due to begin at Christmas 2023.

Doctor Who has often been celebrated for the considerable flexibility of its format, a factor that James Chapman points out in his cultural history of the programme (2006). It is a show that can reinvent itself in a rich variety of ways, not least by 'regenerating' its lead actor and casting new supporting regulars, but also by involving whole new production teams periodically. At its very beginning in the 1960s, though, *Doctor Who* was planned as a bridging programme; a show that could carry BBC One audiences of the day from *Grandstand* through to *Jukebox Jury*. It was to be a BBC 'loyalty' show, retaining a mass audience for the broadcaster all-year-round (Chapman, 2006). This is something which seems particularly fitting, given the extent to which *Doctor Who* has become a flagship BBC brand across the past few decades, even being articulated with the BBC's recent 100th celebrations.

And, as a bridging show back at its very inception, *Doctor Who* also had to be designed to hold the attentions of a family audience but without speaking down to children, as its first producer Verity Lambert was keen to assert:

> I have strong views on the level of intelligence we should be aiming at... *Dr Who* goes out at a time when there is a large child audience but it is intended more as a story for the whole family. And anyway children today are very sophisticated and I don't allow scripts which seem to talk down to them.

The very first academic book about *Doctor Who*, published during its 20th anniversary year, noted that as a result the show could be thought of as a "programme intended for children which has become as popular with adults… without losing its child audience" (Tulloch & Alvarado, 1983, p5). Though it was produced by the BBC Drama Department rather than Children's, whether or not the show could be culturally classified as 'children's TV' has become a recurring controversy among its older fans. The strenuousness with which some commentators have denied this reading would seem to indicate that 'children's TV' has been interpreted, hugely problematically, as a marker of cultural devaluation and presumed non-seriousness. However, across its 60 year cultural lifespan to date, *Doctor Who* has been shared between multiple generations. Forming part of an ongoing cultural exchange between adults and children – between parents and their own children – *Doctor Who* might therefore be thought of as *insistently, productively liminal*; that is, not only representing that third (seemingly stabilising) category of 'family television', but also shading and oscillating between being 'child' and 'adult' television. Such liminality and indeterminacy also suggest that, contra to more neoliberal and commercial perspectives on identifiable target markets (and on audiences of all ages as consumer-fans), *Doctor Who* may speak to and serve child audiences without ever entirely splitting 'childhood' into an isolatable demographic or identity. Here, children can be part of a wider public, or a mainstream/mass audience, just like everyone else. Even if certain things are still assumed about what's appropriate for a younger television audience (a lack of sex and gore, for example) then attributes that may be more strongly intended to speak to 'adult' viewers, such as narrative complexity or series mythology, can nevertheless inspire and appeal to children who are watching the Doctor and their travels in space and time.

As a show that insistently mixes, muddles and crosses the cultural lines of adulthood and childhood, *Doctor Who* remains able to operate in ways that perhaps characterise the best of children's TV. For example, it speaks science-fictionally to younger viewers to enable them to work through powerful emotional experiences such as loss:

> Death is… carefully incorporated into the emotional universe of the show… not thrust… thoughtlessly into the dramatic mix, for effect or convenience. It is one of the functions of the cosmology of *Doctor Who*, where death is present but bracketed by the Doctor's capacity for regeneration, that it is especially able to present death to a family audience: to young people for whom consideration of death and loss are challenges to be faced… as they move through transitions and developments linked to maturation. …The *Doctor Who* cosmology enables children in particular to confront…. jeopardy and "loss" in small, irregular, but reliable doses (MacRury and Rustin, 2018, p291).

But *Doctor Who* doesn't just speak to children and adults in ways that can provide a sense of emotional security for both. As a TV show that doesn't draw any strict division between older and younger fans – both can revel in its monsters; both can learn about its encyclopaedic backstories and histories – it doesn't have to be given up by audiences as they age (unlike totemic examples of children's TV, culturally and reflexively defined as such). The result is more than intergenerational shared cultural space; it is a programme partly about the lead character's changing (regenerating) selves that can allow adult fans to remain connected to their child-selves. In short, it "is not backwards-looking nostalgia or regressive longing for a lost childhood/adolescence that makes such media texts valuable. It is the way in which beloved characters and narratives offer an ongoing... 'framework' for playing with generational identity transitions" (Hills, 2017, p228). Such long-running series allow fans to age alongside them, remembering and reacting to all the other incarnations they have been.

Doctor Who might also be thought of as productively liminal in other ways. It has relatively recently been the subject of a deal between the BBC and Disney. This might be seen as an encroaching and increasing level of programme commercialisation, at a moment when public service broadcasting in the UK remains under threat and in an arguably weakened position culturally and economically. However, as Catherine Johnson has argued in relation to *Doctor Who* as a programme brand:

> While it may be tempting to see the adoption of branding as indicative of a broader commercialisation of the BBC and its core programming activities, the picture is more complex than that. ...[B]randing is used by the BBC to manage both its public service and commercial ambitions around the series. Indeed, ...understanding *Doctor Who* as a brand makes it increasingly difficult to untangle its commercial and public service values (2013, p101).

And right now, the show is arguably more tangled than ever, not just occupying a space between children's TV and TV drama (in institutional terms) but *also phasing between public service and commercialised identities*. Johnson further notes that this scenario can't always be neatly tied back to bigger-picture thinking and policy issues:

> While it is tempting to think of corporations such as the BBC as operating as rational structures whose strategies and intentions can be easily read, in practice – particularly in such a large organisation as the BBC – the processes involved in the production of a series such as *Doctor Who* are far more messy, complex and potentially contradictory, as decisions are often made on an ad-hoc basis in response to issues as they arise, with policy or strategy frequently following on from practice, rather than vice versa (2013, p99).

While this complexity is important to remember (i.e. a big part of post-2005 *Doctor Who* becoming defined as a brand was due to how its own production team approached it, and what people like Julie Gardner and Russell T. Davies wanted the show to achieve), we also need to hold on to certain consequences of public-private blurrings, and associated rightwing governmental attacks on public service TV. One is the ever decreasing amount of funding available to children's TV, specifically. Current (and former) *Doctor Who* showrunner Russell T. Davies has recently reflected on the show's spin-off, *The Sarah Jane Adventures*, which was produced by BBC Children's (2007–2011), arguing that a similar spin-off is no longer viable for the broadcaster:

We're coming back to a world in which money in children's is in even shorter supply... Even with all the good will in the world, we'd find it very hard to do now, unfortunately. ...You also have to keep the spin-offs looking as good as the main show, in order to maintain the entire brand – that's part of the problem as well... There is no plan at the moment for children's, and I'm sad about that, but just affording it would be hard (Davies in Berriman, 2023, p81).

Here, then, brand consistency is cited as an obstacle to extending the success of *Doctor Who*'s liminal character directly back into children's TV production: it would simply cost too much to enable a BBC children's TV extension of *Doctor Who* to keep up with the Joneses of the Bad Wolf/Disney 'parent' show.

That said, *Doctor Who*'s contemporary and heightened blend of public service and commercial forces has seemingly underpinned an unusual approach to the show's forthcoming anniversary – we're getting a series of specials which bring back a much-loved partnership of actors (David Tennant and Catherine Tate) as if to give the mass/mainstream audience what they want within a consumerist ethos, and at the same time this raises innovative narrative questions within a public service ethos of difference and, ironically, non-repetition: the programme has never re-invented itself in quite this way before. How and why has the Doctor regenerated back into an 'old face'? And with the casting of diverse actors, both in these specials and beyond – particularly in the form of the new-new Doctor Ncuti Gatwa – this liminally public service/commercial spirit continues the Jodie Whittaker era's commitment to reshaping *Doctor Who* as an "*inclusive brand*" (Cherry, Hills & O'Day, 2021, p6), less centred on white male identity than previously.

The liminality of the current *Doctor Who* also raises the question of its child audience as fan-consumers, perhaps just as much as older fans, albeit typically without the scale of disposable income. Positioning the imagined child audience as consumers rather than citizens, or uneasily hybridised citizen-consumers, has been viewed as one of the dangers of overtly commercialised children's TV.

References

Berriman, I. (2023). 'Five Children and Smith'. In: *SFX* magazine, 364(April), pp.76—81

Chapman, J. (2006). *Inside the TARDIS: The Worlds of Doctor Who — A Cultural History*. I.B. Tauris.

Cherry, B., Hills, M. and O'Day, A. (Eds) (2021). *Doctor Who: New Dawn*. Manchester University Press.

Hills, M. (2017). 'The one you watched when you were twelve': Regenerations of Doctor Who and Enduring Fandom's 'Life-Transitional Objects'. In: *Journal of British Cinema and Television*, 14.2, pp.213–230.

Johnson, C. (2013). Doctor Who as Programme Brand. In M. Hills (Ed) *New Dimensions of Doctor Who: Adventures in Space, Time and Television*. I.B. Tauris.

Tulloch, J. and Alvarado, M. (1983). *Doctor Who: The Unfolding Text*. Macmillan.

Authors' Licensing and Collecting Society

Think writers should get paid for their hard work?

So do we.

That's why we've paid our members
more than £650m since 1977.

Join today at alcs.co.uk

Is A **Radical Children's Film And TV** Possible?

Dr Noel Brown, Senior Lecturer in Film, Liverpool Hope University

*This article is an extract of a longer article that forms part of an edited collection by the author entitled **Radical Children's Film and Television**, currently under consideration with Edinburgh University Press as part of the 'Children's Film and Television' book series.*

At first sight, the notion of 'radical' children's film and television might seem to be a contradiction in terms. After all, the purpose of children's media, for many people, is to educate, inform, and (possibly) entertain. The Children's Film Department, the forerunner to the Children's Film Foundation (and latterly the Children's Media Foundation), was founded by film mogul J. Arthur Rank with the explicit brief to make films that 'do [children] good', while the first head of the BBC's children's department, Freda Lingstrom, injected an overtly matriarchal sensibility to the long-running *Watch With Mother* strand. If we look at the broader histories of children's media content, this social-developmentalist approach is not untypical.

The basic purpose of censorship, of course, is to 'protect' children from premature exposure to 'adult' worldly realities – violence, sexuality, atrocity, emotional trauma, and so on. In some ways, the protectionist ethos goes hand-in-hand with a long-standing conviction that children's media should be simple, direct, uncomplicated, and innocent (whatever that might mean). At its core, this reflects a widespread belief that young people are not yet competent intellectually, emotionally or behaviourally to deal with the complexities of adult culture and society. Such conceptualisations of children's media typically extend beyond questions of politics and ideology and encompass form and aesthetics, too. Mary Field, the first Executive Officer of the Children's Film Foundation (CFF), argued in favour of children's films characterised by moral binaries ("young children like to think of a world divided into the good, who in the long run win, and the bad, who eventually lose") and a relatively base stylistic approach ("the editing of a children's film requires [...] controlled simplicity and clarity").

In many other countries similar principles of children's film and television as essentially instruments of education have dominated, against which concepts of political engagement or aesthetic complexity appear to be anathema. In Britain, a more progressive agenda emerged in the subsequent work of the Children's Film Foundation in the 1970s and 1980s, and in British children's TV of the same era and beyond (evident in Sir Christopher Bland's BBC report of 1996, in which he spoke of the need for programming that "extends young people's choices and lifts their horizons"). But such content for children, however 'progressive' it may be, stops far short of being 'radical'. So, is children's film and television that could legitimately be described as 'radical' possible? I would argue so – with some important caveats. Firstly, it would be very hard to make a case for the radical credentials of more than a very low percentage of children's media products, much of which is designed to meet the (admittedly valuable) role of educating, informing and entertaining children. Secondly, overt radicalism in children's film and television is considerably rarer than in adult-oriented media, primarily due to cultural expectations and institutional constraints that serve to restrict such content, especially in the commercial arena.

Instead, radical elements tend to operate beneath a cloak of innocence or deniability, couched in allegory or metonymy. In order to protect their livelihoods, their reputations, and even their safety, very few producers, distributors or exhibitors actively choose to draw attention to their radical agenda. In other areas of radical fiction for adult audiences, producers will often signpost the radicalism of the work, not just through the form or political content of the work, but also through marketing and distribution. In the more protected realm of children's film and television, radicalism must often operate under the radar, visible primarily to those who are either particularly receptive – or particularly hostile – to the ideological potential at play (although there are exceptions, as we'll see below).

Thirdly, I would argue that the focus must be on children's film and television that is radical *in context*; in other words, via cultural practices that represent a marked deviation from social, cultural, stylistic, generic or participatory norms. This qualification is important: a Soviet-era propaganda film may seem radical to a contemporary Western audience but otherwise accord with the ideological and aesthetic practices of Soviet-era Russia; *Babe* (1995) may be banned in Islamic countries such as Malaysia (as it was on its initial release) but appear largely innocuous elsewhere. Any consideration of radical works must consider cultural and political contexts, and 'radical' should not become a byword for 'liberal' or 'conservative', 'quirky' or 'unconventional'.

Radical children's film and television, I would argue, falls into three broad categories: 1) content that is *aesthetically* radical; 2) content that is *politically* subversive; or 3) content that is *adopted* for radical purposes by audiences, communities of fandom, or political groups. Let's take each in turn, looking briefly at a few – mostly British – examples. First of all, there is a particularly long history of children's films and television shows that challenge aesthetic norms. The early sound-era German children's film, *Emil and the Detectives* (1931; remade in Britain virtually shot-for-shot in 1935), is one example of a mainstream production punctuated by surrealist visual techniques; the same can be said of some of Disney's iconic 'Pink Elephants on Parade' sequence in *Dumbo* (1941).

However, some films and series sustain an avant-garde aesthetic for their entire duration. The extraordinary Hollywood production, *The 5,000 Fingers of Dr T.* (1953), uses strategies of what narrative theorists call 'dysnarration', presenting a fractured, wilfully obscure, dreamlike structure (with a screenplay by Dr Seuss) of the kind that Bertolt Brecht may have approved. In Britain, such experimental works were considerably thinner on the ground, but ITV's six-part adaptation of Alan Garner's young adult novel, *The Owl Service* (1969), captures much of the formal and political urgency of the late 1960s. A startlingly mature coming-of-age story about teenage sexual awakenings, set against a backdrop of Welsh supernatural folklore, it adopts several cinematographic techniques – most notably jump cuts – that, at the time, were best associated with French New Wave filmmakers such as Jean-Luc Godard; yet it was broadcast in a dedicated children's slot. The Children's Film Foundation, too, was moving with the times: *The Boy Who Turned Yellow* (1972), which marked the final collaboration of Michael Powell and Emeric Pressburger, is full of striking visual imagery and ethereal sounds that align it with avant-garde currents in British theatre, film and television of the period. Although almost vetoed by the CFF board at the planning stages, *The Boy Who Turned Yellow* proved to be a major hit amongst young British cinemagoers, winning a 'Chiffy' award for the best CFF film several times, and it was the first CFF film to be broadcast on terrestrial TV.

Aesthetic experimentation of this ilk has become rare in contemporary Western children's film and TV. However, producers still challenge formal conventions in other ways, dealing with taboo issues usually considered off-limits for children. Scandinavian children's and youth films, for instance, routinely feature representations of graphic sex, drug abuse, and trauma, and engage with complex issues such as suicide, aligning with the French filmmaker Céline Sciamma's conceptualisation of children as young people who desire to be "consumed by an intense narrative". In the process, such works

increasingly destabilise traditional boundaries of children's, youth and adult media.

As noted above, radical political subversion is often more ambivalent in its realisation, particularly in countries such as Britain and the United States, where the mainstream children's media industries operate under relatively tight regulation. The BBC's quintessential children's/family series, *Doctor Who* (1963) is a good example. Although it generally adheres to a broadly liberal worldview, several of its early-1970s serials – particularly those written by former communist party member Malcolm Hulke – present barely veiled assaults on imperialism, advanced capitalism, and race- and class-based inequality, and confront the pressing dangers of impending ecological collapse. In the late 1980s, Andrew Cartmel, the show's script editor, allegedly got the job after revealing in his interview for the position that his aim would be to bring down Thatcher's Conservative government (a fact that caused minor embarrassment to the corporation when revealed in the media years later). Similarly anti-corporate, ecological themes are foregrounded in some of the late-period CFF productions, most notably *The Battle for Billy's Pond* (1976), a film that would have been impossible to conceive during the more middlebrow CFF fare produced under the auspices of Mary Field.

Further afield, children's media has been a vehicle for more explicit forms of ideological protest. The Bengali-language film, *Kingdom of Diamonds* (1980), written and directed by the great Indian auteur Satyajit Ray, is an explicit socialist critique of political and economic oppression of the masses by the ruling elite; in this case, the fictional society Ray depicts stands in for Indira Gandhi's notorious, unilateral 'Emergency' government of the late 1970s. The tendency in post-1980s Iranian art cinema to use child-centred narratives to articulate contentious political criticisms of the theocracy, particularly concerning the rights of women, is yet another example of children's media engaging in political discourse under the cloak of innocence. Such productions, whatever their surface ambiguities, attempt to engage children as active citizens empowered to change the world, whether as social activists, eco-warriors, or other agents of revolution. It is all too easy for critics in Western democratic societies to dismiss or underestimate the radicalism of such productions on account of their allegorical frameworks. However, to do so would be to overlook the fact that the people involved in making content that may be construed as unpatriotic, seditious or heretical risk persecution, exile, imprisonment or worse.

The final category takes as its basis content that may or may not be radical in itself, but which gives rise to radical practices. On the face of it, there's little that is radical about *The Wizard of Oz* (1939), and yet the film – and its star, Judy Garland – have been adopted by generations of queer people; this is just one example of the ways in which oppressed communities might colonise mainstream media content. In the digital age, it is not unusual to find children's media repurposed in playful, ironic, and even shocking ways, parodying or subverting the intentions of the original text. Finally, it's important to remember that many children and young people themselves are avid producers of audio-visual content, often in ways that subvert the very structures and conventions that the (adult) mainstream children's media industry maintains through institutional mechanisms and regulatory control.

These examples give little more than the merest hint of the richness and diversity of children's film and television that challenge accepted social, cultural and aesthetic norms. Kimberley Reynolds, one of the leading authorities on radical children's literature, discusses fictional contributions to "the social and aesthetic transformation of culture" as having "radical potential"; this concept, I would argue, can usefully be extended to children's film and television. This is not to say that children's films and TV with 'radical potential' will necessarily effect radical change in the world-at-large; that would be an impossibly high burden of proof for any work of art. But such works must, at their core, concern themselves with making a critical, potentially transformative intervention in art, culture and society.

References

Brown, N. (2016). *British Children's Cinema: From The Thief of Bagdad to Wallace and Gromit.* I.B. Tauris.

Messenger Davies, M. (2001). *'Dear BBC': Children, Television Storytelling and the Public Sphere.* Cambridge University Press.

Reynolds, K. (2007). *Radical Children's Literature: Future Visions and Aesthetic Transformations in Juvenile Fiction.* Palgrave Macmillan.

Why Don't You... Just Switch Off Your Television Set And Go And Do Something Less Regulated Instead?

Joe Godwin, Former Director of BBC Children's

By 2025, if the BBC gets its way, there will be no broadcast television services providing primarily British public service content for school age children in the UK, a mere 79 years after the first children's TV programme hit the airwaves in 1946.

And the BBC will likely get its way. One of the interesting things about the BBC's announcement to put CBBC 'online' was that there was no outcry. Barely a ripple. No questions in the house, no public revolt like there was at plans to scrap the BBC Singers.

The lack of outcry is partly due to the low visibility of children's content on the BBC. When children's programmes were shown every day on BBC One and BBC Two in single TV homes, politicians, opinion formers and most adults would have been aware of the BBC's offer for kids.

Not now. Kids and parents don't sit down and watch *Blue Peter* or *Grange Hill* together. This isn't due to the disintegration of society and the family; it's simply that in those rosy days of yore, there wasn't any choice. When I was a kid, my media options were BBC One, ITV, horse racing, scrolling pages from CEEFAX, or reading a book! In the '90s I worked on programmes that got huge audiences in the millions. Not because they were the greatest shows on earth, but because there wasn't a lot else for kids to do.

Children have deserted broadcast kids' TV because *they can* – enabled by affordability of technology and, crucially, having control of their own devices. And they really have deserted it – public service linear TV for school age children is watched by a tiny fraction of the nine million potential viewers.

But before we panic and march on the Broadcasting House or Television Centre brandishing our home-made 'advent crown-style' flaming torches, let's ponder whether that would be the right fight.

History is littered with moral panics brought on by young people's relationship with technology and media. Rock and roll on record players, violent American superhero comics, pirate radio stations, predators on Myspace, to name just a few. But history also shows us that one technological advance has never happened – a method for putting genies back into bottles. It's over. It's a shame, but the kids have moved on.

Strategies aimed at *winning back the audience* are almost certainly doomed. And strategies that involve reducing the amount of public service content to bring children back to public service kids' TV are as pointless as they are doomed, a race to the overcrowded bottom.

You may call it a delicatessen, but if it just sells chips, it's a chip shop.

Does public service content for children still matter? If you're a supporter of the Children's Media Foundation or attend the CMC you probably agree it's vital. Our knowledge, experience and instincts tell us that high quality, culturally relevant storytelling for children is one of our most precious cultural assets. It can promote wellbeing, tolerance, learning, citizenship, social cohesion and can encourage children to value culture and crave knowledge. Not to mention the huge contribution kids' TV production and sales make to the UK economy. What's not to like?

I don't think we should despair – yet. This isn't an argument for giving up on offering children well-made, culturally relevant and enriching media. Rather, it's an argument for using our voices and our resources to ensure that public service content for children thrives in a post-broadcaster world. As far as children are concerned, we're already in that world.

What's the answer? One approach would be how the media establishment coped with the challenge of pirate radios stations on ships; seize the ships, outlaw the operators and steal the talent! Sadly globalisation, technology and a lack of appetite for proactive regulation make the 'North Korean' option a non-starter!

Just as all might seem lost, along comes a deus ex machina to save the day, in the form of the Media Bill. A once-in-a-generation opportunity to rethink what we're trying to protect and how best to protect it.

In its current form, the Bill does very little for and says very little about children's content. What it does say is framed in the language of the traditional broadcasters and their public service obligations. Regulation would be, as now, light touch: "do what you think is enough and Ofcom might tell you if it isn't." If you want to know how many hooks public service broadcasters are being let off by this Bill, just note how keen they all are for it to be passed "swiftly".

The Media Bill requires:

> that the audiovisual content made available by the public service broadcasters (taken together) includes an appropriate range and quantity of audiovisual content, contained in original productions, […] that reflects the lives and concerns of children and young people in the United Kingdom […] and helps them to understand the world around them.

It doesn't define "appropriate". The phrase "taken together" means that as long as the BBC does enough, the other PSBs – ITV, STV, Channel 4, S4C, and Channel 5 – are off the hook.

It also states that:

> audiovisual content made available by a public service broadcaster is to be regarded as contributing to the fulfilment of the public service remit for television in the United Kingdom only if the broadcaster has taken steps to ensure that the audiovisual content in question may be received or accessed […] in intelligible form and free of charge.

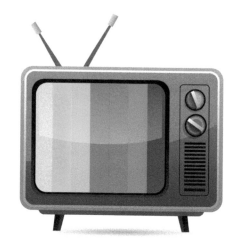

Image: Designed by Freepik

It doesn't count public service broadcaster's children's content on a subscription video on-demand (SVOD) platform, such as Disney+ or Netflix.

And that's nearly all it says on the subject. But I don't think we should use our energies to try to persuade the government to put more into the Bill to regulate public service broadcasting for children. We should focus our efforts on encouraging them to regulate the spaces where children actually are consuming media, not the spaces they've abandoned.

None of this absolves the BBC from its duty to lead the way in distinctive, multi-genre children's content. Without the BBC there will be almost no children's documentary and factual content, and very little British children's drama. The quid pro quo for the BBC is that without distinctive UK children's, the argument for the License Fee is further weakened.

The Online Safety Bill currently working its way through Parliament has bold ambitions to subject global social media platforms to UK regulation. So why not do the same for video on-demand platforms?

Surely some clever person at Ofcom can think of a way to ensure prominence for UK public service children's content on ad-based VODs like YouTube and SVODs such as Netflix?

Couldn't BBC R&D create and licence a 'public service algorithm' that can be shared with VOD platforms so that, if parents and other users want to enable it, their children are served content that ticks the public service boxes – from all content providers?

To help public service broadcasters ensure they're getting the content to the right people in the right places, maybe the Media Bill could set targets for outputs rather than inputs: success measured by hours consumed rather than hours produced?

But above all, the passage of the Media Bill is an opportunity we must seize to remind politicians and our fellow citizens of the true importance of public service children's content to our children and to the UK.

Once the last children have totally abandoned broadcast television, an unlicensed and unregulated children's landscape will be as dangerous and scary for our culture as it is for our children.

CITV: Goodbye Linear

On ITV announcing the closure of the CITV channel, with all children's content being moved to on-demand ITVX, we asked some of those who led the channel to share a few thoughts and reflections.

Nigel Pickard,
Controller of
Children's and Youth
Programmes,
CITV, 1998–2000

Jamila Metran,
Head of Programming,
CITV, 2004–2016

Simon Tomkins,
Manager of Programme
Strategy: New & Future
Audiences, ITV,
2017–present

Steven Andrew,
Controller,
CITV, 2004–2006

Estelle Hughes,
Controller,
CITV, 2003–2006

Vanessa Chapman,
Controller of
Children's and Youth
Programmes,
ITV Network Centre,
1994–1998

What was your best in-house commission at CITV?

NP: Live presentation was a priority to bring cohesion to the daily block and a sense of event. *SMTV* – we took a big scheduling decision and commissioned it for 52 weeks. Frankly that looked like a disastrous decision for the first six months, as the show tanked weekly! But as we now know things worked out pretty well in the end.

JM: The CITV brand was entertainment with a cheeky twist of imagination but mostly it was anarchic. The animated *Mr Bean* was one of my favourites for the channel. He never failed to draw in a big audience and he was popular with both kids and their parents/carers.

ST: *The Rubbish World of Dave Spud*, which is a surreal, funny and distinctly British animation. It's wonderfully brought alive by a great cast. It resonated with a CITV audience as the characters and settings are recognisable.

SA: In the late nineties–early noughties there were a number of transformative commissions; two of the most significant from that time were *My Parents Are Aliens* and *SMTV*. Both shows went on to enjoy enormous success with the audience and provided really solid ratings winners.

My Parents Are Aliens was a high concept family sitcom about three orphaned siblings adopted by two aliens from another universe. The starting point for this show was how can you empower your young characters to know more than the grown-ups. Imagine being able to tell your parents 'whatever you want' and they will largely believe you and embrace it. But the real success of the show was that it was a warm and genuinely funny comedy that explored the rules, rituals and absurdities of what it means to be human and what it means to be a family.

Underpinning the core success of *SMTV* were the hosts, Ant and Dec and Cat. Their warmth, charm and cheekiness were wonderfully infectious and with them as the lead presenters it was always going to be a successful show, but it took a while to find its feet. Initially there was a gap between the aspirations of the show (it wanted to be seen as trendy) and the young audience (5–9 year olds) it needed to serve in order to secure a big audience. The success of *SMTV* required presenters to find the right synergy with the programmes it was featuring – to really connect with that content and show they could share in and celebrate the characters and culture their audiences loved. The significant turning point came with the acquisition of *Pokémon* (the hit acquisition of the late 90s). Ant and Dec embraced *Pokémon* and found a way to put their own spin on it. The other key factor in the success of *SMTV/CDUK* was airing the show 52 weeks of the year, a commitment supported and backed by the then Director of Programmes, David Lidderment, and the then Controller of CITV, Nigel Pickard.

And what was your best acquisition?

NP: Acquisitions are a mixed blessing – of course you need them strategically as you can't afford to have original commissions in every slot, and sometimes you're lucky enough to have a title that is a ratings success rather than a well known 'filler'. But one acquisition in particular contributed to the success of SMTV. For six months we tracked a new Japanese anime series that was hugely successful wherever it launched around the world. I was nervous about the show as it was tonally and stylistically so different to the rest of the schedule, and very commercial! We sent a couple of episodes to the SMTV team for their thoughts on how they might integrate it into the show. They immediately saw its potential and Dec's weekly story update and high pitched "Pikachuuuuuu" is legendary, and *Pokémon* was very quickly a CITV banker.

JM: The Pokémon Company were generous in creating additional content for us to use in our creative campaigns or on-air stunts. For many brands, we were part of an early 360 franchise model required by creators to launch and sustain a successful licensing campaign outside of TV. We were pioneers of that in the 00's and it allowed CITV to keep a place at the table following the HFSS ruling by OFCOM in 2006 [regulating the promotion of products high in fat, sugar or salt].

SA: *Pokémon*. What child wouldn't love the idea of pocket monsters. Wonderfully imaginative, empowering and brilliantly gender neutral.

Also *My Life As A Popat*. A brilliantly wacky family sitcom about a British Asian Family living in London. A kind of Asian *Malcolm in the Middle*. Today, thankfully, diversity, representation and cultural authenticity is very much front and centre of the content being created. Back in 2004, this was not the case. *My Life As a Popat* was the first all Asian children's comedy. It was a joyful celebration of life through the lens of one British Asian family.

ST: *Mr Magoo*, as it perfectly captured the irreverent, anarchic and fun tone of CITV. The disaster-prone antics struck a chord with the audience.

EH: Animated *Mr Bean*, which was commissioned by 'grown-up' ITV and we (and Nickelodeon) were able to acquire.

VC: Difficult to name one, but perhaps a slate of shows from Warner Animation. Including *Pinky and the Brain*, *Tiny Toon Adventures*, and Steven Spielberg and Tom Ruegger's *Animaniacs*. *Animaniacs* was in many ways a game changer in animation; fresh and different, an animated variety show with a mix of slapstick, irreverent gags and pop culture, enjoyed by children and teens alike. But perhaps the most memorable acquisition was the teen sitcom, *Sabrina the Teenage Witch*, which ended up going head-to-head with *The Simpsons* at Saturday teatime, when that first launched on BBC One. There were a few nervous weekends, but thanks to the smart and empowering Sabrina and her wise-cracking cat, it held its own in the ratings and went on to become a firm CITV favourite as well. Who would have thought it?

The best pitch?

ST: Any pitch that matched the high-energy levels of CITV. Also, any pitch that contained the perfect CITV blend of being entertaining, laugh-out loud funny and a little bit gross.

NP: Pitches came into the office at an alarming rate and in all shapes and sizes – someone sent in a full-size car door with programme details scrawled on the panel! Can't remember the show or the producer, just the door! Someone else tried to talk me through a deck whilst we were both stood having a pee in a Cannes hotel – an easy pass!

Pitches varied so much from the full-on, all singing and dancing presentation to the brief outline or script. I preferred the concise pitch – the idea in a paragraph plus an outline/script and any relevant visuals, and details of the key production team.

Difficult to name one best pitch, but *Worst Witch* was an immediate order and from memory was an outline and a script and a phone call!

What were your best moments whilst at CITV?

EH: Saturday mornings at Maidstone Studios for *Ministry of Mayhem*. The excitement of the live show, the fantastic production team and presenters (Stephen Mulhern and Holly Willoughby), the thrilled kids in the audience, and the enthusiasm of the incredible guests when taking part. I'm still not sure if my breakfast with Busted was a dream or not.

VC: When we went for the first time to Toy Fair in New York, presented to the major toy companies, and succeeded in attracting significant ad revenue into the CITV schedule, providing more confidence in the channel and helping its immediate future.

JM: The team wrapped Louise Bucknole (now General Manager Kids & Family, Paramount UK & Ireland - Milkshake! C5 & Nickelodeon) in bubble wrap and sent her through the internal post. It's the kind of behaviour we expected from the characters of our shows, but we actually lived the CITV brand in the office! Wrapping entire desks in newspaper while colleagues were out at lunch, singing karaoke to Simon Cowell as he made his way through the ITV.

SA: Any day the ratings beat the opposition. Watching the producers pick up awards for *My Life As A Popat*, *The Little Reindeer* and *The Giblet Boys* – it's always very rewarding to see something you have believed in being recognised by the audience and the industry.

What do you miss from your CITV days? Any final thoughts?

ST: I miss some of the weird and wonderful discussions, and programme ideas, that would only take place within the world of kids' TV.

JM: I miss the camaraderie and the work ethic of that time. I'm very proud of the channel and what I achieved there. Under pressure, with a very small team and with limited budgets, we adapted, we endured, and we successfully entertained our audience.

I thank Estelle Hughes for choosing me for the CITV Assistant role nearly 20 years ago – back in 2004. I was her best assistant EVER! One dark winter's day she wore odd boots to the office. Nobody told her… except me. Everyone let her limp around on mismatched heels for the majority of the day, but not me. I bravely plucked up the courage to tell her. I'd say that qualifies me as her 'ride or die'!!!

NP: There were shows that didn't work and days we got trashed in the ratings, but looking back there was huge energy and passion across the kids sector. It was a vibrant time with the competition between broadcasters, and producers, resulting in giving the audience the very best UK content. That has to be something we all miss, and today's audience won't experience.

SA: CITV has been the proving ground for some truly amazing talent: writers like Russel T. Davies and Paul Abbot, who both wrote on *Children's Ward*, Jesse Armstrong, who wrote on *My Parents Are Aliens*, and Georgia Pritchett, the creator of *Barking*; and on-screen talent including Ant and Dec, Holly Willoughby, and Stephen Mulhern. Where will the next generation of talent come from? CITV'S demise was inevitable: starved of the resources to adequately compete, it is no wonder it withered on the vine. Where will the stories of the next generation come from, stories that reflect and show the world our children are growing up in, their world here in the UK? The BBC cannot be expected to shoulder all that burden and it's not enough to say "they only watch Netflix". Something must be done to protect their cultural identity.

Image by Freepik

The **Young Audiences Content Fund** – Evaluating The Evaluation

Jackie Edwards, Children's Media Specialist, Former Head of YACF, BFI

For four years, I had the utter pleasure of leading the BFI's *Young Audiences Content Fund* (YACF) – a beautiful initiative funded by UK government via the Department for Culture, Media and Sport (DCMS) to stimulate the provision of public service media (PSM) content for children and teenagers in the UK.

This funding was needed due to the near 75% decline in provision of public service content for children since 2002, when a Communications Act removed quotas and obligations to serve young audiences on public service channels (no obligation = rapid decline in broadcaster investment) and was quickly followed by a series of unfortunate financial events that included advertising restrictions on high fat, salt and sugar foods around children's television and removal of tax credits. The decline of new PSM content coincided with the emergence of huge competition for eyeballs from new digital platforms and saw a migration of viewers to content rich, but unregulated places.

The Contestable Fund Pilot white paper of November 2018 stated that:

> The broadcasting landscape is changing fast. Audiences are engaging with content in a variety of new and different ways. Increasingly viewers and listeners, especially young people, are consuming content online, on smartphones and on unregulated platforms. As the industry changes, it is the government's priority to ensure that the UK's public service broadcasting system continues to thrive. In order to do so, it must continue to provide a diverse offering of high-quality content that its audience deserves.

YACF was the government response to the problems in public service content. As a pilot scheme, YACF was monitored throughout its lifetime. Bigger Picture Research constructed a comprehensive evaluation framework, using a series of metrics against each fund priority (diversity, nations and regions, quality, new voices, etc).

Data captured via the BFI YACF grants software was analysed quarterly – Bigger Picture's regular reporting enabled us funders to be responsive and to make improvements to process and engagement. We knew who was applying and from where, who the team was and if they were fulfilling BFI Diversity Standards, what their projected and actual spend was, how many people they were employing and where, what they were paying people. Along with this quarterly reporting, a much chunkier piece of work was conducted annually – incorporating broadcaster surveys, customer satisfaction surveys from applicants, we asked personal questions about sales forecasts and actual sales, ratings information, awards. Most importantly – via research conducted by Into Film (a nationwide content review of supported shows by young audiences) and Cardiff University (using responses collected via our *See Yourself on Screen* competitions) – we also asked the audience.

The audience appreciated the new content, finding it high quality and appealing, entertaining, informative and representative of their lives and others around them. That was encouraging, given 75% of young audiences report that they don't recognise people that look or sound like them on TV. The detail and integrity of the evaluation process and reporting has built a hugely comprehensive and compelling story of success about the Fund.

The Fund distributed £40.1M in awards over three years, supporting the development of 160 projects and 61 brand new productions made for the young people of this country. 287 hours of public service goodness – everything from current affairs to drama that could be viewed on free to access, safe, regulated channels and platforms and, most importantly, accessible to all.

© Dejan Krsmanović

The Fund proved that a small but specific intervention can make a big difference and deliver real value – the lowest predicted gross value added (GVA) return on investment is £319M (excluding broadcaster funding and factoring no revenue from licensing and merchandise). The Fund stimulated commissions from public service broadcasters. Tax credit increases are nice, but on their own they do not have the impact of targeted funding like YACF on getting public service content actually commissioned. There is also a long legacy tail to the Fund, with productions still ongoing and yet to land, others yet to go to market, and development projects yet to be commissioned.

The Fund supported productions that reflected young lives from all around the country, productions that won ratings and re-commissions, won awards, created jobs, grew careers, improved skills and most importantly, engaged and delighted young audiences. It delivered on its objectives, proved the efficacy of a funding model, delivered social and economic value and demonstrated good value for money. *It is an unequivocal proof of concept.* You can read the full report on the BFI Young Audiences Content Fund site.

The YACF was closed in February 2022 prior to final evaluation and contrary to the initiating 2018 white paper that stated a decision to close, maintain or expand the scheme would be taken following the detailed evaluation.

What now?

The removal of the YACF carrot has meant that PSM commissions for young audiences have returned to pre-fund levels, or worse, with BBC doubling down on 'Fewer, Bigger, Better' and focussing on animation. There is little opportunity or support for new public service television programmes for young audiences in the UK.

Allowing the demise of a public service television offer to our young is dangerous. Left to a diet of cultural influence from everywhere and nowhere in particular, to be exposed to information and news that is not accurate or well informed will diminish their future role as citizens connected to each other and the society they live in.

If we care about provision of public service content, we have two problems to confront: how do we fund it? And where will we put it?

YACF proved that a small intervention can make a big difference and deliver real value in a targeted and specific way. Where such public funding is to be found remains to be seen, but in the scheme of things and for the economic, industrial, cultural and societal value it delivers back (way beyond the initial cash injection) it doesn't seem like a big ask.

Alongside investment, regulatory intervention to motivate commissions would be helpful. The YACF carrot has proved its worth. Imagine a world with a carrot and a stick… But getting new content commissioned and funded is probably the easiest part (sort of). How to get more young audiences to discover this content is the biggie. If there was a new fund, should we open up the qualifying platforms? YACF support was restricted to content intended for free to access, public service, Ofcom regulated platforms. Putting public service content where young audiences are is not a bad idea, but how would it be surfaced and presented – there is much chat around public service algorithms, but there are still safety concerns? How can that be realistically tackled when the extent of the inertia-bound Online Harms Bill is still being haggled over and unknown?

It is of profound importance to reflect our children's lives back to them, to help them understand and empathise with their peers, to explain the world to them, to support their development and to make them feel connected to our society. The questions are complex and the issues many. But our children's media diet should be of concern, it's a big part of their lives and helps shape them as citizens. This needs a bigger conversation. Children should be a political priority for many reasons: their media lives is just one reason, but it's a pretty important one.

Beyond Magic: The Importance Of Stylistic Diversity For Toddlers

Dr Cary Bazalgette, Former Head of BFI Children's Education

Twenty years ago, I was chatting with a group of 9 year olds in a Peterborough primary school, just after they'd seen *The Boy Who Stopped Talking* (Sombogaart, Netherlands 1996). Despite having had to read subtitles, they had been deeply affected by the film, which is about a traumatised refugee child. Conscious of how different it was from what they usually saw, they gave me a trenchant summary of what they disliked about the TV programmes and films that are assumed suitable for their age-group: "we're sick of magic, miss!"

This statement was no surprise to me, given the work we were then doing at the BFI, initiated in discussion with the leaders of the National Literacy Strategy that the Blair government set up in 1998. They were keen for us to try and persuade teachers to introduce school children to non-mainstream films and discuss them in class. Between 2004 and 2007 we published seven DVD collections of non-mainstream short films, mostly not made for children, but nevertheless suitable for different age groups, starting with one for 3–7 year olds (*Starting Stories*, BFI 2004). We provided training sessions for teachers, organised in collaboration with local education authorities. The publishing venture was extremely successful, with wide sales to schools across the UK and collaborations with half of the local education authorities in England.

The teachers' comments on the primary age children's responses to these films were invariably both surprised and enthusiastic. They had found that their pupils were much readier to watch – and re-watch if possible – films that were stylistically very different from what they were used to, and that didn't necessarily yield up all their meaning on first viewing. The children clearly knew much more about moving image media than the teachers had expected. Outcomes that the teachers hadn't anticipated included more confident and fluent talk, extended writing, increased vocabulary and surprisingly pertinent insights.

But soon the roundabout of educational innovations turned again, as it always does. Teachers began to see film viewings merely as a handy way to help them reach their government-imposed targets for children's attainment, rather than as significant cultural experiences that deserve exploration and discussion. The BFI management team decided to make savings by abolishing its publishing department and, by 2010, Michael Gove's ascent to the Department of Education ensured that Matthew Arnold's view of cultural education as "the study of perfection" (Arnold 1869) would thenceforth decide what children read and saw in school.

I had left the BFI by then, but I didn't forget those teachers' and children's responses. When I was a teacher myself, I had internalised the mantra "start where the kids are" – in other words, try to be alert to what their previous experiences may have been. I wanted to find out about the prior learning these children must have achieved, that had enabled them to make such unexpectedly sophisticated responses to the unfamiliar material they had watched. Trying to answer that question made me want to investigate children's very early responses to moving image media. That led eventually to my PhD research and my book *How Toddlers learn the Secret Language of Movies* (2022), both of which draw on a video-based case study, observing my twin grandchildren's viewing practices between the ages of 22 months and 40 months, and coming to recognise what a crucial period this is for learning how to make sense of TV and film.

It's not surprising that research on this age-group, which I'll refer to as toddlers (in contrast to research on infants or preschoolers) is relatively rare, and often badly designed. Many 2 year olds' spoken language is hard for anyone outside their immediate family to understand; their behaviour in new environments is very unlike their behaviour at home, and they are notorious for their unpredictable behaviour, changes of mood and strong wills – at least in Anglophone countries, where the term 'terrible twos' is in widespread use. Anyone who really wants to try and understand anything as complex as 2 year olds' responses to moving image media has to observe them in their home environments, preferably using video to capture the 'data'. Analysis of the children's observed responses not only has to draw on extensive knowledge of child development, but also on the knowledge of those who know them well, i.e. their parents or grandparents. It's not surprising that some of the most influential studies of this age-group have been done by family members themselves.

This ideal research method would be expensive to commission and is likely to be time-consuming. So, if producers of TV series for toddlers (i.e. post-infant, but pre-preschool) want to get evidence that their programmes appeal to the audience, they are likely to seek researchers who produce evidence that is easily observable. That this is a standard assumption about good practice in studying young children may be inferred from Blum-Ross and Livingstone's otherwise excellent paper *The Trouble with Screen Time Rules* in which they point out that research on children's video-viewing rarely or never "recognises children's pleasure in singing and dancing along with a video, or enacting the drama on the screen also with their siblings in front of it" (Blum-Ross & Livingstone, 2018, p183). It's nice to see kids behaving like this, but to imply that it's important evidence for establishing the value of what is being watched reduces potential audience research on preschool TV to a version of Gogglebox.

One of the most striking findings of my research was the massive investment of energy that 2 year olds are capable of investing in their self-driven efforts to make sense of something that is different from what they are used to and that they do not yet understand fully. I first saw this when I was simply minding the twins (then aged 22 months) while their mother was getting the dinner ready. I impulsively reached for one of our BFI DVDs, picking a short animated film that

I thought they might like: *Laughing Moon* (Nishimoto, Japan 2000). Nishimoto uses the black geometric shapes of the Tangram game to form a succession of figures: a chicken, a rock 'n' roll guitarist, a dinosaur, a dog, etc. Each figure engages with a little round yellow shape (the laughing moon) that keeps morphing into different objects – a ball, a bird, etc – and evades each character's attempts to catch, throw or kick it, laughing as it escapes. The final figures are two motorcyclists who assemble the two halves of the 'moon' and the remaining Tangram pieces into a motorcycle but after roaring away they crash it, die, and float up to heaven. When the film started (with a loud pop as the 'moon' emerges from a black box) both twins stopped what they were doing and stayed immobile and tensely attentive for the six minutes of running time (far longer than most adults can manage – just try it!), and then immediately asked to see it again. But dinner was ready, so we didn't see it again until they were at my house two weeks later. Again, the twins watched it intently, starting to get the 'project' of the film, which is to use sound effects (clucking, rock music, roaring, etc) to help identify each austerely simple Tangram figure, and they were looking excitedly at me as they recognised each one.

*Watching **Laughing Moon** for the first time, aged 22 months*

During the 20 months of my research, I showed the twins several other films from the 16 available in the BFI *Story Shorts* series and from the collection of 12 in *Animagine*, published by the Film and Video Workshop in 2010.[1] One or two that were sad or a bit disturbing they watched attentively but did not want to watch again; others became favourites for several weeks. They soon became adept at choosing films from the thumbnails on the DVD covers, which in each case gave them a glimpse of the style as well as the subject matter. They still enjoyed the mainstream TV and DVD material that they watched at home, having moved on from *In the Night Garden* to *Peppa Pig*, *Baby Jake*, *Tree Fu Tom* and many others. What became clear to me as I studied their responses and preferences was that when they were immediately and intensely attracted to any new programme or film, it was not because of the content, for example "helping them to understand the world" or "seeing their lives on screen" (neither of which is usually apparent in the first two minutes) but due to innovative stylistic features that appealed to them: for example, how characters and settings are presented; how information is given and withheld; how time-frames are conveyed and managed; the relationships between sound and image. Toddlers can't articulate this (and most 9 year olds can't either) but we can tell by their

---

[1] All these resources in the BFI Story Shorts and the Animagine collection used films that had had no other release except, in some cases, on Vimeo or YouTube, and were selected from festivals by our researchers. Rights were negotiated with small production companies or the filmmakers themselves. Short film and animation festivals present a potentially huge and underexploited source of wonderful material for very young children.

choices and their attentiveness that they do notice innovation when they see it. We can also infer their approval by their continued curiosity and loyalties, and by the further choices they make as they move on (if they get the chance) to more narratively and stylistically challenging material once they have 'used up' their old favourites.

Could it be that the demand for observable responses may at least be contributing to so many producers of TV for toddlers being trapped in the iron grip of requirements for cute, brightly-coloured, smiley characters (big- or dot-eyed), OTT presenters, singalong music and repetitive narrative devices? Google 'best TV programmes for toddlers UK' and you will get a top seven that consists of *Peppa Pig*, *In the Night Garden*, *Hey Duggee*, *Bing Bunny*, *The Octonauts*, *Twirlywoos*, and *Sara & Duck*. Individually these are all lovely shows, and children obviously do enjoy them, but collectively they – perhaps not including *In The Night Garden* – demonstrate a depressingly narrow range of stylistic norms. This lack of stylistic variation is endorsed by parents who are nervous about vague but threatening admonitions such as the '2+2 screen time' rule, so are inclined to try and find 'more of the same' for their toddlers to watch. I believe that this is seriously under-serving the needs of toddlers. Encountering generically and stylistically diverse material is an essential introduction to any cultural form. If it is introduced too late, children will be less inclined to try it, so this kind of diversity is perhaps more important for toddlers than for children of 3 and over. Many picture-book publishers know this: children's media producers should too.

*Watching **Animatou** for the first time, aged 28 months*

The significance of toddlers' dedication to understanding moving image media is that it is part of what has always been their main task in life: becoming an independent individual who can survive and grow up. In the modern world, this has become even more challenging and complicated than it may have been in ancient societies, given the vast range of information and entertainment sources that are now part of

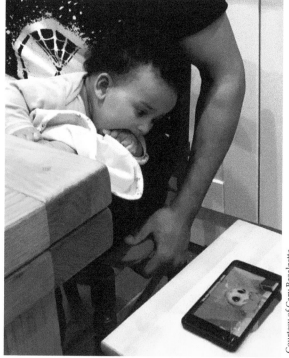

the social and cultural environments that they need to understand. What toddlers have always done, all the time, is learn. They are never not learning. The third year of life is a crucial time in which individuality is established, and everything they encounter contributes to that process. This is why I find it shocking that so little attention is paid to this age range in the discussion of children's media and that, apart from ensuring the delivery of harmless fun, there is so little debate about the importance of stylistic diversity.

What agencies have the scope and remit to help change this situation? Ofcom's activities as a regulator with a remit from government include making sure that "a range of companies provide quality television and radio programmes that appeal to diverse audiences." This is pretty broad, but it seems that "quality" for the 0–3 age range primarily means "harmless" as far as Ofcom is concerned. And although it does important and fascinating research on how children and adults consume and relate to media, it does not study children from when they start watching moving-image media, which for a large proportion of them is at around 3 months old (Marsh et al., 2005) or maybe younger, given that smartphones became widespread after Marsh and colleagues did their research.

The titles of Ofcom's *Children's Content Review* and of the Young Audiences Content Fund make it clear that style is not their concern. Their focus on content alone meshes with a wider characteristic of public discourse about media, that refuses to consider 'the media' as cultural forms whose genres and styles are worthy of serious attention. I used to joke that whoever thought up the name of the Department for Culture, Media and Sport was under the delusion that these are three separate things. They are not: media and sport are both cultural sectors, vital contributors to how we recognise, imagine and remember ourselves and our lives, our histories and our futures. The ways in which information is given, stories are told, images are constructed and games are played do matter, as we all know. The *Children's Content Review's* demand for "original, high-quality programmes" has little to say about what "original" and "high quality" might actually mean, although in their own ways, my 2 year old research subjects and the Peterborough 9 year olds clearly had their own versions of those concepts in mind, even if they could not articulate them, when they chose what they did and did not want to watch.

An apparently intractable problem for creative people in the UK children's TV industry is that their work is not only aimed at one of the two social sectors that are still powerless to resist being stereotyped in everyday discourse (young people; the other being old people), but is also in a despised form, not usually even recognised as 'cultural'. There is just one agency whose remit shows that it should be trying to change this: the BFI, whose Royal Charter requires it "to encourage the development of the *arts* of film, television and the moving image throughout Our [sic] United Kingdom, to promote their use as a record of contemporary life and manners, to promote education about film, television and the moving image generally and their impact on society, to promote access to and appreciation of the widest possible range of British and world cinema…" I highlighted "arts" in that quotation because, apart from its appearance in BAFTA's title, television particularly is almost never referred to as an art, and film only rarely: the word 'media' is often assumed, in many quarters, to be separate from, even in opposition to, the arts – as I have discovered in many consultations, meetings and projects throughout my career. The result of this separation is that the stylistic features of television (especially children's television) are rarely discussed in mainstream reviews. This is probably the main reason why toddlers' need to learn how to understand the media is so widely ignored. Perhaps this is a challenge that the Children's Media Foundation might address?

References

British Film Institute (2004). *Starting Stories*. BFI Royal Charter, https://www.bfi.org.uk/strategy-policy/bfis-royal-charter

Bazalgette, C. (2022). *How Toddlers Learn the Secret Language of Movies*. Cham, Switzerland: Palgrave Macmillan.

Blum-Ross, A., and Livingstone, S. (2018). "The Trouble with "Screen Time" Rules". In G. Mascheroni, Ponte, C. Jorge, A. (Ed.), *Digital Parenting. The Challenge for Families in the Digital Age*. Goteborg: Nordicom.

Film and Video Workshop (2010). *Animagine*.

Halliday, M. A. K. (1975). *Learning How to Mean: Explorations in the Development of Language*. London: Arnold.

Marsh, J., Brooks, G., Hughes, J., Ritchie, L., Roberts, S., and Wright, K. (2005). *Digital Beginnings: young children's use of popular culture, media and new technologies*. Retrieved from Sheffield: https://www.researchgate.net/publication/265183910_Digital_beginnings_Young_children%27s_use_of_popular_culture_media_and_new_technologies (accessed 08-11-2021)

Piaget, J. (1928). *The Child's Conception of the World*. London: Routledge and Kegan Paul.

Weir, R. H. (1970). *Language in the Crib*. The Hague: Mouton.

'Scary, But Fun': Children's Explorations Of Digital Risky Play

Denise Mensonides, PhD student, Centre for Media and Journalism Studies, University of Groningen, **Dr Anna Van Cauwenberge**, Associate Research Director, Ipsos European Public Affairs Team, Belgium and **Dr Marcel Broersma**, Professor of Media and Journalism Studies, University of Groningen

Lucas and Benjamin (pseudonyms) aged 10 and 9 respectively, like to play the digital game *Minecraft* together at the afterschool location they both attend. *Minecraft* is a popular video game in which players find raw materials and can build structures. Players can play the game in two settings, 'creative' and 'survival' mode. In the creative mode, players are given supplies to build the structures they want to make. However, in survival mode, players must find their own building supplies and food, and are at risk of encountering different creatures, such as skeletons and zombies. Lucas and Benjamin both enjoy playing the game in the survival mode and select this setting together before they start playing. While Lucas enjoys fighting the monsters, Benjamin is more frightened when he encounters a skeleton. He says he wants to 'get out of here' and starts to panic a little. Lucas stops his game and watches how Benjamin tries to flee while giving him directions of where to go. He directs him to the house they built in the game and Benjamin uses this safe space to hide from the skeleton. Finding refuge in their safe space, Benjamin relaxes again and laughs. When the skeletons disappear, Benjamin comes out and picks up the game where he left off.

Thrilling digital games, such as the horror games *Doors* and *Piggy* on *Roblox*, an online game platform, are very popular among children in primary schools. These games often revolve around 'scary-looking' characters which children must fight or hide from. Kids interact with these games in different ways, ranging from playing these games themselves to watching videos of others playing on YouTube, or making paper drawings of the game characters. While children seem to enjoy engaging in these thrilling and somewhat scary experiences, parents and teachers are often worried. What if the characters in these games cause children to have nightmares? As a consequence, many parents have chosen to delete these types of horror games and restrict their children from watching videos that include scary characters on platforms such as YouTube or TikTok. This observation, however, raises the question whether shielding children from these types of content and scary digital experiences is the best way to help children develop resilience and skills to adequately deal with risky digital encounters?

Our research explored how Dutch children between the ages of 8 and 12 engage in 'digital risky play', i.e. when playing online thrilling or scary games. We found that children actively create and shape a space in which they feel they can safely experiment with digital risky play, for example by turning on lights, playing with friends, or adjusting technical settings. These tactics not only allow children to experiment with thrilling encounters, but also facilitates feeling safe and empowered, and the development of resilience. This is crucial for children to cope with risky digital encounters now, and later in life.

When designing our research, we first took a step back and conceptualised 'risky play' and the functions it may serve in children's development. Risky play is an enjoyable and thrilling or exciting activity that allows children to take risks, for example by climbing trees or cycling fast. By

engaging in this type of play, children are exposed to risk and risk-assessment. By climbing trees, for example, children learn that the situation might take a turn when they end up too high, making it difficult to safely get back down and possibly leaving children feeling scared. By engaging in such activities, children playfully explore their own boundaries, while also developing tactics that help them return to a safe space when play becomes too scary. What children experience as 'thrilling' or 'scary' depends on various factors, such as age or personality. This means that children engage in risky play in different ways. For some younger children cycling fast could be described as risky play, while for older children this might not be the case.

When we talk about 'risky play' we often refer to outdoor play, of which climbing trees is one example. However, in our study we found that children experience similar thrilling feelings and

photoroyalty from freepik

encounter risk and risk-assessment in digital play. Many children were found to engage in digital risky play by browsing what they call 'somewhat scary' games on *Roblox*. There are many different games from which children can choose on this online game platform that are marketed as 'horror games' for all ages, or ages 9 and up. The games are very popular, not only among children, but also among YouTubers who make 'gameplay' videos that are based on these online games. Children were found to engage with these games by playing them with friends or siblings, watching videos on YouTube about the games, or when talking with peers about their thrilling experiences playing them. However, children do not only engage in digital risky play when playing traditionally 'scary' games, but also when experiencing thrilling situations in more creative games such as *Minecraft*.

In the case mentioned in the beginning of this chapter, we observed both boys enjoying playing *Minecraft*, even when Benjamin became scared when he unexpectedly encountered scary-looking characters. Indeed, when asked to describe how they experience digital risky play, many children in our study referred to it as 'scary, but fun'. This is the core of digital risky play: it allows children to experience risks and feelings of fear while still allowing them to enjoy the activity. To keep it a pleasant experience and not become overwhelmed with scary feelings, children were found to use different tactics. We distinguished four categories of tactic that children use to navigate digital risky play: technological, physical, emotional, and social.

In the case mentioned earlier, Benjamin uses technological tactics to create the house in the game, to which he can flee when he finds that the game is becoming too scary. Other technological tactics include switching between different 'creative' and 'survival' modes and adjusting the brightness of the screen or the volume of the game. Such tactics allow children to gain more control over their playful experiences and actively create an environment in which they feel comfortable to experiment with and explore playful risky digital situations. To shape such an atmosphere, children also employ physical tactics outside of the game, such as turning on the light in their room. This also works the other way around: turning the lights off when children want to create a more thrilling environment for their digital play. Other physical tactics include using their arms as shields or peeking through their fingers, allowing them to gradually engage in this type of play.

Benjamin and Lucas also use social tactics to navigate digital risky play. They find comfort in each other by building the house together as a retreat strategy and talk through thrilling situations by leading each other to this safe space. When playing together or discussing experiences with peers, parents and teachers, children learn to contextualise these risky experiences, as well as take advantage of the technological skills and tactics friends may have already developed. Closely linked to social tactics are emotional tactics. These tactics are mainly aimed at building resilience through desensitization, stress-reduction, and by relativizing and reflecting on experiences. For example, if children feel that playing a specific game might be too scary, but they still want to engage with it, they familiarize themselves with the characters by drawing them or looking up still images of the game. And if a game becomes too scary, they actively search for 'nice' and 'funny' games to counter the scary games and unwind, almost as a detox strategy. By employing emotional tactics, children both emotionally prepare themselves for playing a risky game, as well as avoid content that could lead to feelings of fear.

Developing these four types of tactics through play is an iterative process. Every time children engage in digital risky play, they not only improve their ability to use various tactics, but also learn about their own boundaries and how to deal with potential boundary-crossing experiences. They feel in control of their digital risky playful experiences by deploying these tactics. Furthermore, these tactics allow children to feel at ease playing again (repetition) and to engage in a way that is comfortable for them (e.g., by first drawing the characters).

As children spend an increasing amount of time using digital technologies and are exposed to different types of risky experiences through digital technologies, it is important that we empower them to develop tactics to manage risky digital encounters. We, therefore, argue that digital risky play is an addition to offline risky play. It allows children to develop strategies that can aid them in dealing with both physical as well as digital risks. This does not mean that all risky experiences are good experiences. If play becomes too scary it might lead children to become fearful for long periods, not wanting to engage in digital risky play at all. It is therefore of the utmost importance that this type of play, albeit being led by children themselves, is supported by friends or parents. Supporting children in their explorations of their own boundaries through risky playful content requires a balance between creating a supporting and safe (digital) environment, while also granting children the agency to shape and engage in digital risky play.

So, the next time you encounter children playing thrilling or even scary games, ask them how they navigate these risky situations. You will see that they employ a range of tactics to keep their play 'scary, but fun'. After all, we wouldn't forbid children to cycle or climb trees.

This work was supported by the Dutch Research Council (NWO) under grant number 410.19.008.

Child Rights By Design

Prof Sonia Livingstone and **Dr Kruakae Pothong**, Digital Futures Commission and LSE (London School of Economics and Political Science)

Children's rights in a digital world are rising up the public and policy agenda. This has consequences not only for governments but also for the providers of digital products and services. Business as usual is no longer sufficient. Whether positively to do the right thing, or to avoid the problems of getting it wrong, providers are increasingly asking themselves how to make their products and services more compatible with children's diverse needs, thus realising (and not abusing) children's rights.

But not every digital provider fully grasps the nature and significance of children's rights or how to apply them in practice. Designing and developing for children's rights is especially challenging for mainstream providers – including CEOs, innovators, product managers, designers, developers and marketers – catering to the general public. With all the talk of designing with children's best interests in mind, how can one go about it? And who needs to know what?

Designing with children's best interests in mind

> "All businesses that affect children's rights in relation to the digital environment [should] implement regulatory frameworks, industry codes and terms of services that adhere to the highest standards of ethics, privacy and safety in relation to the design, engineering, development, operation, distribution and marketing of their products and services … and take measures to innovate in the best interests of the child." (*General comment No. 25*, para 39)

The formal adoption by the UN Committee on the Rights of the Child in February 2021 of *General Comment 25* on children's rights in relation to the digital environment was a game changer. This statement provides authority, clarity and direction on how the UN Convention on the Rights of the Child applies to the work of all stakeholders whose actions are within its scope. That includes those who provide digital products and services for children. And it includes those whose digital products and services are likely to be used by children, as part of a broader market, whether or not children are among the intended users. It even includes those who provide products and services that children don't use directly but that impact on them (think of cameras in public places, school information management systems, health databases or parental control tools).

By design

> "The idea of 'by design' harnesses the generative power of providers, designers and policymakers to shape technological innovation in ways that prioritise values that promote human wellbeing – privacy, safety, security, ethics, equality, inclusion and, encompassing all these, human rights including children's rights." (Livingstone and Pothong, 2021)

For digital businesses, a 'by design' solution is widely advocated – think of safety by design, secure by design, privacy by design and others. A 'by design' approach avoids the expensive and difficult task of retrofitting design to respect rights after a product has already been developed. It brings crucial benefits by being in the vanguard of emerging standards and regulations, building trust, and preventing reputational risks. Further, with increasing concerns about attention-grabbing digital business models infringing children's rights, 'risky by design', even 'deadly by design' are obviously to be avoided.

Beyond anticipating and preventing problematic infringements of users' rights, what should businesses do? The Digital Futures Commission has asked, what does good look like for children, recognising that while it is important to address safety, security and privacy, there is a risk of neglecting children's other rights and the crucial balance needed between different risks and opportunities for children living in diverse circumstances. We have previously advocated 'playful by design' for digital providers of services with which children can and do engage playfully. In our latest work, we build on this, widening our lens to embrace all of children's rights as they apply to all digital products that may affect them.

Child rights by design

> "It's 100% a design decision. It's quite easy to make a game that just goes on infinitely. It's more of a decision to go, actually we're going to stop it… We could make that game last for ages, but we took a decision that actually 30 seconds to a minute is long enough… We've got a different objective to the game rather than just [kids] playing." (A small digital content and game developer for children)

Even with good intentions, catering for children's best interests and their rights in the digital context is not easy. Some, especially small companies, can feel like they are flying blind.

> "When we design for preschool toys, we've got a lot of guidance… I've been designing all my life, but when it comes to the digital, I would say I would not know where to look… I would not know the limits of designing for a kid." (Independent digital designer)

Child Rights by Design offers a fresh direction, and a principled vision, to inspire innovators to realise children's rights when designing digital products and services. It is grounded in the United Nations Convention on the Rights of the Child (UNCRC), the most widely ratified international human rights treaty ever, applicable to all children from birth to 18 years old. We also drew on the combined wisdom of about 100 relevant policy documents, national and international.

We worked collaboratively with all kinds of experts – designers, developers, lawyers, technologists and researchers from small, medium and large businesses – and we consulted children and young people – always the best part. They emphasised their agency, first and foremost, and the importance of trustworthy support from adults that is responsive to their needs and has their best interests in mind.

> "But [children] also have the right not to be exploited… so … digital services' terms and conditions… should be easier to understand what they are… They should just make it a really short sentence that is quickly run through." (Year 8 school student, Essex)

> "We have the right to speak up, and people should listen." (Year 7 school student, Yorkshire)

> "Can you make more apps based on Toca World? Because it is so creative for lots of children – so they can do something creative instead of watching something." (Year 3 school student, Greater London)

Children also called for more support from industry, though they have learned to be sceptical of receiving it, which is why they seek creative workarounds, being fascinated by specific product features and how they help or hinder their activities, enabling adventure and participation or compromising safety or exploitation.

To cut a long story short, we mapped all the articles of the UN Convention on the Rights of the Child, and all the provisions of General Comment No. 25, and distilled 11 design principles, as shown below. We added design cases, relevant laws and regulations, suggested design resources and input from children and young people.

Working again with designers and developers, we also mapped the 11 principles onto the Design Council's Double Diamond, highlighting 'stop and think' questions for each phase of the innovation process. We concluded with a checklist – how to keep all the principles in mind, identify what's already good, and figure out the next steps needed. If the 11 principles serve their purpose, companies using this toolkit will effectively be conducting a child rights impact assessment – itself becoming more popular in digital contexts.

CHILD RIGHTS by DESIGN PRINCIPLES

1. EQUITY & DIVERSITY
Do you treat all children equally, fairly and support vulnerable children?

2. BEST INTERESTS
Are children's best interests a primary consideration in product design?

3. CONSULTATION
Are children meaningfully consulted in developing your product?

4. AGE APPROPRIATE
Is your product appropriate for child users or adaptable for different ages?

5. RESPONSIBLE
Do you review and comply with laws and policies relevant to child rights?

6. PARTICIPATION
Does your product enable children to participate in digital publics?

7. PRIVACY
Have you adopted privacy-by-design in product development and use?

8. SAFETY
Have you adopted safety-by-design in product development and use?

9. WELLBEING
Does your product enhance not harm children's physical & mental health?

10. DEVELOPMENT
Does your product enable children's learning, imagination, play and belonging?

11. AGENCY
Have you taken steps to reduce compulsive and exploitative product features?

Child Rights by Design shouldn't be seen as a tick-box exercise but an exciting road map. For although we don't promise all the answers, we are confident of the direction of travel – one which will help you discover the answers that are right for companies and rights respecting for children.

For more, visit the microsite at https://childrightsbydesign.digitalfuturescommission.org.uk/ and read here https://digitalfuturescommission.org.uk/blog/child-rights-by-design-our-guidance-for-innovators-toolkit-is-finally-here/

SAFFRON CHERRY IS PROUD TO SUPPORT THE CHILDREN'S MEDIA FOUNDATION 2023

Directing Children

 Geoff Coward, TV Director, and Creative Director for Playa Digital

Directing children is one of those skill sets that no matter how long you've been doing it, you learn something new every time. Often the methods you use one day won't work the next. Kids are of course unique individuals and that's what makes them such brilliant, engaging, fun people to work with. Some of them have great comic timing, some are incredible at improvising and others would rather be doing anything other than whatever it is you're filming. Although there is no 'one size fits all' approach to directing kids, there are some hard-and-fast rules – and a few tips that I've picked up along the way.

Safeguarding

I'll start with this, as it's the most important. Safeguarding the welfare of children on a shoot is a huge subject in itself, but if you're directing kids you're at the sharp end of it all. There's risk assessments, licensing, chaperones and restricted working hours all to consider before you even step foot on set. The BBC's child protection 'Ten Golden Rules' code of conduct for working with children is a great way to remind you of best practice when you get there.

With so many sophisticated methods of finding information online such as reverse image searches, remain alert to avoid possible jigsaw identification, where someone could connect various pieces of information to identify a child beyond what you intend.

Once your programme is broadcast, the footage will be out there forever. Could your footage be easily adapted or misinterpreted? Shot sizes and composition go a long way to keep context within a scene.

Schedule

Working with younger children takes longer, yet ironically you'll have less time available to work with them. You need to give kids time to get used to their surroundings and explain things clearly and simply to them. Often the schedule is tight, so you'll need to be as efficient as possible when it comes to filming. Make sure you've marked out the whole scene and done any head scratching before the children arrive on set. Bear in mind you may need to adapt your plans depending on how the children are responding and of course once you're ready to call action, one of the kids on set (closely followed by the others) will decide it's the perfect time for a loo break.

Crew

Working regularly with the same crew helps as you'll already have a shorthand with them. (I know a number of DOPs that always have sticker eyes in their pockets ready to put below the lens if we need a child to look at the camera.) Being able to communicate quickly and discreetly with the crew will enable you to minimise the formal, often loud dialogue that goes with location and studio filming as this can seem intimidating and confusing. If you can, keep the conversation on set down to one voice that is focussed on the child; they'll be far less distracted and hopefully more comfortable in their environment.

Staging

The best way to get a good natural performance from a child is to make their action natural. Stage the scene so their path is the most obvious one to take. The children you're filming with will trust you if you make sure they understand what they're doing and why. Give as few instructions as possible so they can focus on the most important parts of the scene. Once you've got the nuts and bolts of staging in place, you can add actions and emotions. If you don't need the audio at every moment of the take, then talk them through it if necessary and keep quiet for the dialogue. Try and keep out of view or they might be tempted to look at you for reassurance.

Coverage

Does the child need to be there for the whole scene? You don't want them getting bored or to eat into those precious few hours they can work on set. Once you've covered the child's dialogue and action, can someone stand in for the child (or maybe sit in for the correct eye-line) while your other performers record their part of the scene? Some dramas and sitcoms have content that is not appropriate to perform in front of a child even though the story requires their presence. You'll often see these parts of the scene are shot in close up while the child's reaction has been shot separately.

Courtesy of Geoff Coward

Directing children and audience shots

If you're doing a multi-camera shoot and you need coverage of kids in the audience, don't just keep one camera back from the main action to hunt for shots. If you have time, do a pass of key moments where all the cameras are looking at kids only. Those perfect shots you've seen of kids laughing / dancing along / cheering may have been caught during the main performance, but the chances are they're a pick-up. Make sure the cameras have lenses long enough to pick out individuals – it's lovely to have a group of kids all reacting together, but inevitably one of them will be doing something completely different or inappropriate! Don't be tempted to use a less experienced camera operator for the audience shots, finding great reactions of kids. Knowing who's going to react and when is an art in itself.

Group shots

It may be that you want to shoot a group of kids performing something complex together – such as singing or dancing to a recorded track. With any luck you'll have a group that's well-rehearsed and know their routine inside out. However, if you have a complex or long continuous set-up where one mistake means you're going back to the beginning, consider compositing the participants together. This is simple on green screen where you can film each child separately or in small groups and then in the edit put them on a background together (and if timing is key you can play back the previous kids' recordings as you record the next ones). Alternatively, you could do a simple split screen where you lock-off the camera and place the children in different areas of the frame, but film each child separately – as the background is identical in each shot, it's a simple job to blend each child (with their perfect take) into one master shot. If you have the budget, motion control cameras can do a repeatable moving version of the same thing.

Distractions

Make sure no monitors are visible to children on set even with a static image on – this includes Autocue, unless they're actually going to use it. If you notice your young contributor staring intently at something while you're talking to them, they've probably found the eight-inch reverse scan monitor the puppeteer is using underneath the dining room table on the other side of the studio. Keep visible crew on set to a minimum, as it can be intimidating having all those grown-ups staring at you. If it's a big shoot, use screening for the crew to wait behind, watching monitors until they're needed.

The key ingredient

With all the complexities and constraints around filming with children, try not to forget the key ingredient – they're children. Kids identify with the characters you bring to the screen, whether they be human, animations or puppets. How you treat these characters both on- and off-screen can really affect the children that know them well. Take the time to think about how your actions might look from their perspective. An exhausting day at work for you is an exciting, possibly once in a lifetime experience for the children you're working with – try to make it a good one.

Design Considerations For Kid-Friendly Virtual Influencers

Dr Sonia Tiwari, Researcher, College of Education, Penn State University

Miquela Sousa is a 19 year old pop star featured in Time Magazine's 25 most influential people on the internet.

CB is a teenage boy with over three million followers on Instagram.

Shudu is a supermodel and social media sensation who has worked with brands like Vogue, Balmain, and Samsung.

What's common among these social media celebrities?

They are not human. They are virtual influencers!

Virtual influencers (VIs) are computer-generated characters who are designed to mimic the behavior of human influencers to engage with audiences on social media platforms. According to VirtualHumans.org, there are currently more than 200 VIs on social media. While most of the existing VIs focus on advertising and marketing aimed at young adults, they can also provide entertainment, education, social commentary and advocacy for other age groups.

The popularity of VIs has surged in recent years, as is evident from a 2022 survey conducted by the Influencer Marketing Factory. The survey revealed that more than one-third of participants had made purchases based on recommendations from virtual influencers, while 58% of respondents admitted to following at least one virtual influencer. The majority of VI followers are in the 18–24 age range.

After being fascinated by the VI phenomenon for a few years, I wondered: "What if we wanted to design kid-friendly VIs?" With the advancements in generative AI tools and the metaverse, the potential of VIs in the children's media industry looks promising. Following this curiosity, I began a research study while teaching at the California College of the Arts in San Francisco. My primary question was: What factors should we consider while designing kid-friendly VIs?

As part of this research, I studied social media influencer market reports, analyzed content of VI accounts on Instagram in 2022, and conducted interviews with children's media experts. Based on this research, I recommend the following five design considerations for designing kid-friendly VIs:

1. Character and storyverse

Think about the *who*. Who is the VI? What makes them unique? What's their story?

Successful VIs are unique and detailed, just like characters from other media such as books, films, TV shows and games. Children can form a parasocial relationship with their favorite character, especially when these characters act as conversational agents with a two-way communication (Hoffman et al., 2021). VIs lend themselves to this type of parasocial relationship with children because they communicate on social media in a first-person voice and connect with followers through comments, messages, or live sessions.

Since VIs are essentially well-developed characters, consider following the classic principles of character development from the worlds of fiction writing and visual design: recognizable visual style, relevance to and representation of the target audience, a unique personality with specific quirks, a development arc over time, a strong backstory, expressive voice, relationships with other characters, etc. The storyverse (sometimes called story-universe or storyworld) includes all the characters, environments, plotlines, sub-plotlines, and other story elements around the VI.

From a marketing perspective, kid-friendly VI characters typically follow specific brand archetypes such as: creator (imaginative, artistic), caregiver (nurturing and compassionate), innocent (happy, optimistic), or jester (silly yet relatable).

2. Content

Think about the *what*. What will the VI share with their followers? What ideas, stories, images, videos, etc?

Since VIs primarily exist on social media, the content is usually bite-sized and focused on themes that are relevant to the followers. Consider creating a social media calendar to plan the content in a variety of formats: images, carousels, GIFs, short videos, etc. VIs could also benefit from following the classic 3Cs of children's media: the child, context, and content (Tiwari, 2020a). What is the age range of your target audience? What do they care about? What is their context? Customize your content to those needs. According to my research, kid-friendly VI content could include age-appropriate silly humor, cute GIFs that capture character personality and inspire small positive actions, positive quotes and images, characters interacting with each other and their environment in micro stories, seasonal content addressing contextual issues, cultural celebrations, seasons, milestones such as birthdays or first day of school, ASMR short videos that help relax, informal images and short videos about the VI's everyday life that could help children understand the VI more closely, not to mention behind the scenes and making-of content for caregivers and educators to earn their genuine buy-in to the concept of the VI.

3. Experience

Think about the *where*, *when*, and *how*. Where, when, and how will the followers engage with the VI?

Consider designing a 'Transmedia Suite' (Tiwari, 2020b): a collection of content designed for various platforms, devices and formats. Consider which *platforms* are better suited for children and which for their caregivers and educators. For example, child-facing content could be delivered on YouTube and Roblox, but caregiver and educator-facing content can be delivered on Instagram and TikTok. Consider which *devices* your audience will be using, such as tablets and television for younger children (ages 5–7), and mobile and desktop for older children (ages 8–10). Explore different *formats* such as short videos, GIFs, DIY, and Games.

The VI could also host their own website which gives the VI backstory and key calls to action (CTA), houses links to all social media accounts, offers additional resources like articles, projects and freebies, and allows the community to reach out to the VI and the team behind it.

Consider going beyond screens (Tiwari, 2022) with prompts for VI-themed offline activities for children. When thinking of 'how' the VI would engage with followers, consider addressing in a first-person voice follower requests in posts and comments, hosting LIVE interactions such as virtual concerts and hangouts, replying to personal messages or forum questions, etc. The VI could also offer opportunities for joint media engagement (Ewin et al., 2021), such as by prompting children to do some activities with their caregivers or designing games that can be co-played with adults.

4. Ethics

Consider the *why*. Why does the VI do what they do? What ethics guide their actions?

Consider designing culturally sensitive, health-conscious, data-safe and developmentally appropriate content. Since there are no clear legal boundaries around VIs specifically, it may be easy to hide behind a VI and deliver inappropriate content without the fear of consequences. An ethically designed kid-friendly VI should involve inputs from diverse experts such as child development professionals, educators and researchers. Since VIs typically produce fictional versions of real human life (e.g. characters that are going to school, spending time with friends and family or specific hobbies), children may be prone to the ELIZA effect (which refers to the tendency of people to attribute human-like qualities, such as intelligence or empathy, to computer programs that engage in conversation with them). Children may develop strong (parasocial) relationships with VIs, which may be a good thing only if the humans behind the VI have strong ethics.

5. Monetization

Consider the *which*. Which part of the VI experience will cost followers money?

Not all VIs are designed to be monetized, some merely exist as a form of creative expression or advocacy. However, when considering monetization for kid-friendly VIs, it would be helpful to think in terms of which specific experiences, products and/or services might be genuinely useful for children, caregivers, and educators. Consider designing a sliding-scale of monetization, or the freemium model where some features are free, and others may require payment. Make these payments available under parental control so that kids do not accidentally spend money while interacting with the VIs.

I recommend offering thoughtful experiences to kids, caregivers, and educators – such as educational virtual tours with VIs, lesson plans for integrating VI-based curricula, VI-themed age-appropriate toys and games, or the ability to customize VI to promote creativity and representation. Whether or not these value-based offerings *should* be monetized depends on the goals and intentions of the organization or individual behind the VI.

Kid-friendly VIs – potential uses

While kid-friendly VIs may seem like a promising revenue stream for businesses selling products to children, their potential is much wider. From individuals to organizations, kid-friendly VIs can potentially benefit the children's media industry in a variety of ways.

1. **Repurposed VIs:** Existing characters from other media such as film, television, gaming, toys, and publishing could easily become VIs. The switch could involve creating short-form content suited for social media, using a first-person voice to interact with children, and sharing more informal and non-performative content that would help children get to know the character more deeply. VI content may also work as a testing ground for existing IPs to expand their storyverse, based on early fan responses.

   Popular kid-friendly IPs such as *Bluey*, *Peppa Pig*, *Minions*, and *Angry Birds* could easily pick one of the characters and turn them into a VI – sharing their life with fans in a first-person voice.

2. **Studio-backed VIs:** Large studios could design a new kid-friendly VI exclusively for social media platforms, since they already have access to the talent pool and financial resources to conceptualize, produce and launch any character-themed IP such as VIs. These VIs could serve specific goals such as building communities, advocating for issues that the creators care about, promoting a product or service, or creating partnerships and collaborations.

   Brud, the studio behind Michaela Sousa, also designed other VIs following the same design language and established them as friends with each other. This example shows that it may be profitable and convenient for studios to figure out a production pipeline that works for one VI and then replicate on other VIs.

3. **Indie VIs:** Since VIs generally share images and short-form videos on social media that do not require the kind of time and resources typically needed for film, television or games – it may be possible for smaller studios, nonprofits and indie creators to develop VIs at a low cost. With the advancements in generative AI, creators can train and co-create with AI based on their original artwork and story ideas. This could significantly speed up the production process that otherwise requires larger teams, more time and greater resources. VIs could offer excellent creative expression opportunities to indie creators.

For example, photographer Cameron James Wilson created Shudu to increase representation of black women in high fashion, and Loryn Brantz created the Good Advice Cupcake to share her sense of humor and positivity with Cuppy's followers. In both these examples individual artists were able to express themselves creatively through a different medium.

In conclusion, whether you are a children's media organization with existing IP that can be repurposed as VIs or a solo creator thinking about designing new kid-friendly VIs – here are five elements to consider: a relatable character design; relevant content across multiple platforms; thoughtful experiences that can be experienced online and offline, solo or with adults; ethics such as designing culturally sensitive, health-conscious, data-safe and developmentally appropriate content; and monetizing thoughtful products or services for children, caregivers, and educators.

References

Ewin, C. A., Reupert, A. E., McLean, L. A., and Ewin, C. J. (2021). The impact of joint media engagement on parent–child interactions: A systematic review. *Human Behavior and Emerging Technologies*, 3(2), 230–254.

Hoffman, A., Owen, D., and Calvert, S. L. (2021). Parent reports of children's parasocial relationships with conversational agents: Trusted voices in children's lives. *Human Behavior and Emerging Technologies*, 3(4), 606–617.

Iconic Fox. (2022). *Brand archetypes: A guide to understanding and using brand archetypes*. Retrieved from https://iconicfox.com.au/brand-archetypes/.

Influencer Marketing Factory. (2022). *Virtual influencers survey infographic*. Retrieved from https://theinfluencermarketingfactory.com/virtual-influencers-survey-infographic/

Tiwari, S. (2020a). Understanding the 3Cs: Child, Content, and Context in Children's Educational Media. *TechTrends*, 64(3), 348–350.

Tiwari, S. (2020b). Transmedia Making Experience Design: Framework to Design Learning Environments that Connect Media with Making. In *Proceedings of the FabLearn 2020 – 9th Annual Conference on Maker Education* (pp. 150–153).

Tiwari, S. (2022). *Across and Beyond the Screens: Investigating Children's Joint Engagement with Educational Media and Related Activities*. The Pennsylvania State University.

'10 Minutes Of Hello': Writing For Preschool

Vanessa Amberleigh, Executive Producer and Script Editor

Writing for the preschool audience is fun, variable, eye-opening, challenging and doesn't have to be done in crayon. In fact, if you do want to join the many talented writers that produce amazing scripts for the youngest audience, get yourself Final Draft! (Yep, the script programme used worldwide and even on grown-up TV.)

I have written, produced, edited and presented multiple preschool scripts for most of the major broadcasters in my very long, happy career in children's television.

I was fortunate to start in TV under the mentorships of Cynthia Felgate and Anne Gobey, two amazing women who knew their craft and more importantly what appealed to the youngest viewer. (Cynthia was the Exec Producer of *Play School* before going on to set up Felgate Productions which produced *Playdays*. And Anne Gobey was a producer for *Play School*, *Playdays*, *Caterpillar Trail*, the first ever director on *Play Away* and brought Floella Benjamin to our screens.)

So why have I called it '10 minutes of hello'?

When I was first introduced to writing for preschoolers, generally scripts were 25 minutes long; apparently that included 10 minutes of hellos, 10 minutes of goodbyes, and a 5 minute song in the middle. Yes 'hello' and 'goodbye' is very important to the youngest audience (if you've ever seen a presenter wave at the end of a children's show a young viewer will wave back at the TV) but this summary slightly undermines the complexity, understanding, simplicity without being patronising, fun, imagination and knowledge of your viewer that is essential to write a script for preschoolers – without mentioning the usual script requirements of understanding character, strong narrative, three act structure and 'where's a good place to put the song?'

And, no pressure, but you are writing for the audience with the best imaginations in the world.

So where do you start? Maybe you are working on a series that has happened before so characters, structure, format, songs, etc. are already established and in this case let your imagination fly, but ensure that you only tell the story that is relevant to your characters. Remember, this young audience has a very limited experience and knowledge of the world, therefore many of the stories that writers use may well be the same: the surprise birthday, hide and seek, lost voice, undiscovered artistic genius, something about a hat, a picnic. There is always the 'potato' and 'yellow' script (don't ask)!

If you are writing for a brand new series, it will be exciting as you will be part of developing character, catchphrases, humour, structure as well as tone and heart.

Never forget that the audience you are writing for are very impressionable and what you write may have a huge impact on their lives. Everyone can probably remember a storyline, character, visual action or song that has stayed with them forever.

So not only does what you script have to use language that is relatable to our audience – and that can be reflecting the early stages of dialogue or help teach them correct language – what the characters do by their actions is also equally as important. As scriptwriters you are as integral to your characters' actions as the director – be it live action or animation.

There is a big difference between a 1 to 3 year old and a 4 to 6 year old in their comprehension and ability to regulate their actions. Hopefully, as a script writer you will know which age group is your focus. (If this isn't made clear to you by the production, ask!)

Up to the age of 4 a child is very egocentric. They do not understand empathy and will always put their needs and wants first. As scriptwriters you can help enlighten them and guide them to what empathy, the understanding of other peoples' feelings, means and the importance of empathy in society.

Once children start to integrate in the classroom, be it nursery, preschool or school, they begin to realise that sometimes what they want to do isn't always the most important thing. This is where they enter 'gang phase', especially around the age of 6, when they actually start to think less about themselves and more where they fit, how they want to fit in and reflect the gang they are playing with.

So if you are writing a script for preschoolers ensure you are very clear on the age group you are talking to or reflecting in dialogue. It can have a big impact on your success and the success of a series.

Never underestimate the power of actions that are written into scripts. A little question I ask myself when I look at action is "would I like to see a 3 or 4 year old repeating this action unsupervised?" If the answer is "no", and quite often it is, then come up with another idea or a very clever way of ensuring that the viewer (who is probably watching this without a grown up close by) understands that the action being portrayed should not be replicated by them.

Other considerations: Is your script appealing to generic learners or specific? Do you want to appeal to the three main groups of learners, auditory, visual or cognitive? Could your script stand out by appealing to one of those groups?

As grown-ups, we take simple things for granted that we need to be careful of for preschoolers. For example, don't forget 'please' and 'thank you'. How many times a day do we say "please" and "thank you" and yet in preschool scripts, where this should be so important, it is often neglected? So try to model best practices with pleasantries, best behaviour and safety. (Yes, it is Ok for a baddie to wear a cycle helmet and apologise for their naughtiness!)

Going back to the limited knowledge of the world, make sure the script you are writing could only happen to those characters taking part and only happen in that environment. 'Surprise Party' is a great script but just because you've written it for one set of characters, don't lift and shift for a new set. And don't forget humour; it is so, so important for this age group. This is the age group that will roll around the floor hugging their tummies laughing out loud because they've seen a bouncy ball bounce around a room or seen someone struggling to get into a tiny pair of shoes – slapstick is their favourite type of humour but fraught with imitative behaviour pitfalls! Don't rely on word play, the youngest audience love the sound of silly words but don't understand puns. And even if you are writing about what we as adults consider serious subjects or dry subjects, don't feel that humour will not enhance the experience for the youngest viewer.

I could write pages and pages about scripting for preschoolers but as the writer you need to feel that what you are delivering will bring a smile to the face of the youngest audience, help inform and inspire, and resonate with them now and in the future.

Hopefully your script will be the one that they quote, chuckle about and reflect on throughout their childhood and grown up life.

Good luck. Happy writing!

Building Teams To Build Authenticity

Kyle Jenkins, Acquisitions and Programme Director, Commissioning Executive, Milkshake! C5

We often talk about diversity as if we've cracked the code. With more diverse characters on screen, it's easy to believe that the work is done, however, increased visibility on screen is just the first hurdle in a race towards authentic representation across the children's media landscape.

With the built-in responsibility of educating and preparing our audiences for the world, children's content has always moved the needle forward at perhaps a greater rate than our counterparts in adult programming, yet we've still only scratched the surface in creating truly authentic representation.

The word representation is key here.

While we may showcase or include characters and contributors from a wide range of backgrounds and experiences, are we truly representing them? It's here that the issue of authenticity comes into play and we must ask ourselves if we are being true to the experiences of these characters and what we can do to ensure that our stories are being told by the right people in the right way.

Our audiences tell us directly when something hits (or misses) the mark, and we often find that the most authentically created stories and characters are the ones that resonate most with our audience. This isn't a new concept, it harks back to the adage of 'write about what you know', but how do we ensure that we build teams with a diverse enough range of experiences to ensure that the stories we're telling reach marginalized audiences while appealing to the wider demographic?

It's all about who's in the room. What may at times have felt like a box-ticking exercise, is now paying dividends as we see a show's development made unquestionably better as a result of authentic hires being made at every level. As such, we're seeing stories and characters rooted in truth, created by people with lived experience rather than people who, as Rebecca Atkinson, the creator of disabled-led preschool series *Mixmups* put it, *"told the stories through a prism of their own perception of what it was like to be disabled"*.

Mixmups is a prime example of authentic production processes in action, as while the show was created by a disabled person and the majority of the production team have lived experience of disability, it isn't a show about disability. We sometimes forget that while they all have different experiences of the world, all kids find joy in magic, adventure and play and that's exactly what *Mixmups* is about. The fact that most of the core cast are disabled needn't be consistently flagged.

Framing the series in this way allows the series to appeal to all children while giving disabled characters a platform to carry a series without having to explain or exploit their disability. This affirmative model of disability representation celebrates its characters regardless of their abilities, and the magic of their world and the strength of their friendships are what shine above all else.

It could be argued that this would have been a less likely outcome from a production team with no lived experience of disability, resulting in a baseline negative approach, which more often than not, paints disability as something the characters are trying to overcome or have fun in spite of.

As broadcasters, it should be a comfort to be able to trust a production team to handle subjects in which some of us have very little lived experience. While intentions may be good, there is no amount of goodwill that could produce a series that so effectively centralises a group of disabled characters and not their disabilities.

Editorial feedback still stands, from a brand and storytelling perspective, but even here things are flagged that challenge our thinking and create a deeper understanding of the experience of the very people we're trying to represent and entertain.

It may not be realistic or always appropriate to crew up an entire series around a particular experience or background in this way, but it always comes back to who's in the room. What story are we trying to tell and who can best support that story being told effectively? Whether it's finding the writer who is best positioned to tell a particular story or bringing in a consultant to review the work, it's about who can comfortably represent that character and their experience or can tell that story in a way that doesn't patronize, misrepresent or oversimplify.

Working with the National Autistic Society on the 'How Can I be Friends with Theo?' episode of *Daisy and Ollie* allowed us to tell a simple story of preschool age children learning about autism in a non-pressurised way.

The script, which followed the show's existing format of answering some of the inquisitive, wacky and sometimes difficult questions we're often asked by preschoolers, used Theo's autism as a backdrop to a story that's ultimately about friendship and how to make friends with people who may be different to us. As such, the episode takes a much more nuanced approach that feels both informative and age-appropriate and, again, would likely have been trickier to achieve in the hands of people without a lived experience of autism who may have more heavy-handedly signposted the issue.

It's clear that the key to authentic representation is the diversity of thought found in the spaces where decisions are made. The echo chambers that are generated in rooms where there is a shared perspective and experience reverberate far too loudly across the industry and the disruption of inclusion is the clear way to literally change the narrative.

Producers who welcome this diversity of thought tend to create projects that carry more weight. Not to say the projects become more agenda-driven by any means, but that awareness of the benefits of engaging marginalised audiences tends to strengthen the idea as the audience has truly been considered.

In a series like *Reu and Harper's Wonder World*, a series we commissioned from black-owned production company Doc Hearts, we see our preschooler hosts Reu and Harper Grimwade, first seen on Milkshake! in *Go Green with the Grimwades*, embark on a series of playdates with children from a variety of different backgrounds. By welcoming Reu and Harper into their homes to teach them about their traditional customs, culture and the universal language of play, we see a prime example of authentic and representative storytelling. Here, our diverse array of contributors are able to control their narrative and provide Reu, Harper and our audience with real world takeaways that aren't translated through an intermediary that doesn't have the lived experience of said cultures. Being created by a team who have the necessary sensitivities to develop and produce such a series is key to the show's success.

Courtesy of Kyle Jenkins

Reu and Harper's Wonder World

Diversifying the voices in senior positions in the industry and actively implementing the existing initiatives that are in place is as important now as it was when the events of 2020 shook the world awake. We have the tools we need, it's now a matter of using them effectively.

The benefits of diversity and inclusion (D&I) intervention and more inclusive ways of working are clear and while there's work to be done, it's important to celebrate the wins. Hearing of Rebecca Atkinson's journey from Disability Programmes Unit trainee to the Exec Producer of the first disabled-led preschool series is a testament to their importance.

Comfort Arthur's journey to becoming an episodic director on the BBC's *Jojo and Gran Gran* by way of on-the-job training, made available through the *ScreenSkills – Make a Move* training program, helped to fill a gap for a black episodic director on a series centered around black culture and characters.

Tito Olawole's entry into the BBC Ignite scheme has seen her successfully progress through to the final stages and as a result has her own anime inspired series in development.

It's not a perfect system but the talent is there, as are the resources which will support ongoing development.

Keeping the cultural, societal and material benefits of more inclusive working practices at the forefront of our minds is key to continuing the upward trajectory and we must also continually remind ourselves who we're doing it for. Every email we receive from a viewer thanking us for including them or someone who looks, sounds, walks or talks like them should be enough of a reminder; now we just need to get on with it.

Thanks 'Bandit' (I Think!): Representation Of Fathers In Children's TV

 Nigel Clarke, Presenter and Founder of *Dadvengers*

The representation of dads in UK children's media has come a long way over the years. Gone are the days when dads were portrayed as 9–5 workers who only came home from the office moments before the kids went to bed. Nowadays, we are definitely seeing more and more positive and accurate portrayals of dads in our TV shows, movies and books. It's taken quite some time to get where we are, but the question I still ponder is whether there is enough of it?

Having worked in children's media for 25 years and watched it for over 40, I have seen the representation of dads change. Add to that the fact that I set up *Dadvengers* to enable dads to feel more supported as parents and you'll understand why I feel the need to take a long hard look at dad representation both now and over the years.

Never before has the behaviour of men been under such scrutiny and the way we see ourselves in the media affects how we behave day-to-day. It may sound dramatic but it's similar to the debate around boys playing aggressive video games, and then behaving aggressively in the playground or with friends. If our children see dads that are not massively engaged all around them why should they be inspired to grow up to be engaged fathers themselves.

What dad representation was around when I was a child?

Being an 80s' child, at first it was quite difficult to actually remember portrayals of fathers from that era. And upon looking deeper I think it's because I don't think family was depicted much in children's content. I remember shows like *Bric-a-Brac*, *Fingermouse*, *Let's Pretend*, *Pigeon Street*, and reruns of *Bagpuss* and *Mr Benn*. All great shows, but none, bar *Pigeon Street*, fully depicted a family, or a dad. And even then I don't remember the dad being involved much. It's not that men weren't in these shows, just that none were depicted as fathers, even though some could be seen as father figures.

With that in mind I have to bring father figures into this conversation, to get a feel for what I was seeing as a child. The only shows I could think of that had men in them who might fulfil the father figure role were *Play School* and *Sesame Street*. And quite surprisingly both had black men in father figure roles, which, looking back, was ground-breaking. Especially when you see the way the media has portrayed black men in the fatherhood space since.

Image by Freepik

What's the difference now?

The difference now is that there are more programs telling the family story. From *Peppa Pig* to *JoJo and Gran Gran* to *Bluey*, we now have rich examples of family life on screen. Naturally we want this to be representative of real family life, but also paint an aspirational picture for those watching.

What is really noticeable when you look at the changes, is that the representation really reflects what was going on in society at the time. So in the 80s it was considered the norm for men to be the breadwinners in a family and women to be at home looking after the family. Therefore most of the TV shows made then don't focus on dads being around.

Nowadays, a dad spending time at home to help with the kids, being in touch with his feelings, and exploring his and his children's mental health, is something we are talking about a lot more, and striving for. Hence you now find shows with dads like Bandit in *Bluey*. Which, in the case of the very engaged and playful Bandit, has dads wondering if they will ever live up to a new standard being set. *Bluey* shows the power of children's media to inspire adults, and I have listened to many a dad talk about the ideas and help that *Bluey* has given them with their own children.

Why it's important to keep pushing for even more reflective content

Shows like *Bluey* are just the beginning; we need to keep the momentum going. Just like us, our TV shows need to evolve and help normalise the things we see all around us. Though we are in a better place, there are still aspects of our lives that are not represented. If we are to live up to the claims we make about our shows being diverse and inclusive, we still have a way to go.

Where are the shows that have a single father? Where are the shows that have a truly blended family? Where are the shows with same sex parents? Where are the shows that depict male emotional expression? If they are out there, they aren't prominent enough. And what's really sad is that I bet shows like these have been talked about in development and pre-production over the last few years but, somewhere in the process, someone or some organisation has got cold feet and toned things down. It always happens. Just so people don't rock the boat or appear to be too ahead of the curve. But if we are going to encourage our children to be better parents than us, to be more open, to be more aware of other people. We need bold adventurous content making, by content creators who are willing to risk short term profit for change making content. It's easier said than done, it takes more research, it takes more time, but we owe it to ourselves, and we owe it to our children.

Image by Freepik

The **Changes And Challenges** Of The Faces Of Fatherhood

Laura Sinclair, Doctoral Researcher, School of Journalism, Media and Culture, Cardiff University

Parents are ever reliant on children's television as a platform for learning and still place trust in public service media to educationally entertain their children within a safe place. But what about us adults? In some instances, it could be argued that children's television is as much for the adults as it is the children. As I sit and watch CBeebies early in the morning with my toddler, I often find myself just as immersed (or sometimes more so!) in the narratives of the animated worlds imagined. As a parent countless questions run through my mind around my child's consumption such as "is this educational?" and "how long is an acceptable amount of television for him to watch?", but I am also very often left questioning the representation of parental roles and what this means for us adults and the parents of the future, our children.

Whether parents are a considered part of the production process or not, the presence of parental roles and the representation of parents is important to both children and adults. Martin and Ruble (2004) identify children as 'gender detectives' (2004, p67) who are gathering information about gender cues to better understand how to socialise within their social circle and perform their expected family roles, and this could also be applied to parents too. How parents are represented is just as key as the representation of the child characters, as this meaning-making process contributes towards children's understanding of gendered roles, division, and labour within a family household.

Historically, parental roles have appeared to be shown as less progressive in terms of gender, but this slowly seems to be changing, particularly when representing fatherhood in recent years. Fathers have often been represented as incompetent and not undertaking parental duties to the same standards set as the female characters, with this often softened for comedic value; for example, see Homer Simpson. But has this contributed to a conflicted attitude toward fatherhood? What does this mean for both the adults and children watching?

Father's displaying active involvement in their child's narrative within children's television is often centred around playfulness and this is beautifully demonstrated within Australian cartoon *Bluey*, recently branded 'a bible for modern parenting' (Lamont, 2022). Bandit, the father in *Bluey*, appears to be the hero of modern fatherhood with his fun-loving imaginary play with his daughters Bluey and Bingo often dominating the episodes. Bandit is shown spending a lot of time in the home, but his character also highlights the difficult child juggling work-life balance (particularly in the episode 'Rug Island')

and demonstrates the guilt that many parents feel. However, it also seems that such imaginary play provides Bandit with escapism from adulthood and its realities. Due to its enlightening representation of parenthood, *Bluey* has achieved cult status and has captivated the adult audience, with even an adult made for adult listener podcast, *Gotta Be Done – A Bluey Podcast*, listened to worldwide.

Whilst undertaking my doctoral research, I have noted this trend and movement towards fathers displaying 'boisterous affection' in some television programmes. This behaviour is demonstrated by, for example, being noisy, tickling, and spinning children around whilst, in contrast, mothers are often shown closely embracing their children in somewhat of a calmer manner on screen. This 'boisterous affection' can be thought of as a mixed display of fatherhood and masculinity where fathers can display their physical strength and love that could be deemed as more acceptable whilst negotiating their masculine position within the family, which sums up where we find ourselves with representation on screen. To some extent, this can be seen within the *Bluey* episode 'The Pool'. Bandit, Bluey and Bingo take a trip to the swimming pool, Bandit forgets to take the sun cream and armbands branding them "boring", but soon realises upon arrival to the pool that the children cannot swim without them. Chilli (Bluey's Mum) is then seen arriving with the "boring things" to make Bandit and the children's fun possible. Although just one small example, this highlights that the representation of the fun-loving father still presents some issues and a level of fatherly inadequacy. Within Gotz et al's (2008) study of children's fantasy worlds, the scholars stated that 'boys are torn between traditional and new images of manhood, conflicting messages, and expectations' (2008, p136), remaining strong and in control whilst also showing affection and emotions. It seems that the realities of fatherhood and its representation on screen continue to still be doubted to some extent.

Offering positive, aspirational role models that construct a narrative around fatherhood – that offers kind, loving, attentive fathers that are actively involved in shaping their children's lives – benefits both child and adult viewers. The small children watching these programmes base their meaning-making of the world through such consumption and children can be receptive to stereotypical expectations that circulate through media messaging. *Hey Duggee* plays a part in adding to a positive fatherhood narrative to fatherhood. Although not a father himself within the series, being a visible, male lead character in a care providing role (within a nursery) should be celebrated. *Hey Duggee* also challenges stereotypes and boundaries on gender and family structure, which is a refreshing change for parents and children alike. Progressive and representative fatherhood roles are aspirational and freeing for young boys, in helping to move away from restricting, conflicting, and often confusing, masculine messaging.

Bibliography

Gotz, M., Lemish, D., Aidman, A. and Moon, H. (2008). *Media and the Make-Believe Worlds of Children: When Harry Potter Meets Pokemon in Disneyland*. New York: Routledge.

Lamont, T. (2022). The cult of *Bluey*: how a kids' cartoon became a bible for modern parenting. In: *The Guardian*, 11 Jun.

Martin, C. L. and Ruble, M. (2004). Children's Search for Gender Cues: Cognitive Perspectives on Gender Development. In: *Current Directions in Psychological Science*, 13(2).

Children's Mental Health And Media:
Tools For Talking About Feelings

Laverne Antrobus, Consultant Child and Educational Psychologist, The
Tavistock Clinic and Portman NHS Foundation Trust

*Ashley Woodfall met with Laverne to discuss children's mental health, and her work with
BBC Children's and Sky.*

Laverne's 'starting point' was in the clinic where she has been meeting with a lot of young people
presenting with issues like anxiety, depression, low mood – and through creating pieces on BBC's
Newsround and Sky's FYI she has looked to help children understand mental health, as well as
establish the building blocks for them be able to openly discuss their wellbeing.

Children have been particularly concerned by issues like climate change, Coronavirus and racism
(especially in the light of the Black Lives Matter campaign), and Laverne's approach, working with
the teams at Newsround and FYI, has been to offer children 'top tips' to address the issue-at-hand.
Providing a "framework to think" through, Laverne distils four or five key points that respond in
some way to children's worries.

The pieces have proven popular with children, as they have allowed them to digest key information,
but they have also left an opening for parents or other trusted adults, and this is something Laverne
is keen to do in her work – to "hook it back to parents". The pieces also tend to end with a little task,
encouraging children's self-advocacy and enabling discussion at school, with friends and with family
– getting children to feel that they are more than passive observers.

As a psychologist, Laverne has been able to say, "yes, there are legitimate things to be worried about,
let's not deny it". But at the same time she could introduce information that feels both helpful and
'soothing'. Children's anxiety has been going through the roof, but acknowledging that something
like the pandemic was completely new to us and everybody was worried, healthily legitimised those
anxieties and reassured children that what they felt was a natural response to a significant issue in
their lives – that they would benefit from being able to address and talk through.

Laverne is concerned that children are accessing news from what might not be trustworthy
sources. For example during the pandemic, children, like adults, sourced information that was
often contradictory or misinformed. Through her work she has been able, when addressing hard
issues like the Coronavirus or BLM, to say "look, this is coming from a trusted news source" and

"just take a bit of care with how you find your news". Laverne reminds us that "we're working with very young, vulnerable minds" – one click away from finding content that might be deeply unhealthy for their wellbeing.

Children benefit from hearing and talking about mental health and the important issues in their lives – and how they might impact on each other. It helps mental health become more 'ordinary' and 'accessible', that "there is something called low mood and that this can affect lots of people". It can give children "a window into what might be happening in their own families", offering a framework to understanding and a language with which to open up conversations.

Photo by Artem Kniaz on Unsplash

The Rez: The Origin Story Of A Children's Media Mental Health Intervention

Dr Martin Spinelli, Professor of Podcasting and Creative Media, University of Sussex

In the summer of 2018, just after we'd submitted the manuscript for our book *Podcasting: The Audio Media Revolution*, Lance Dann and I sat down with Tim Pilcher of the comics press Soaring Penguin Press to brainstorm a new project. Lance and I wanted to do something different. Our publishing history had been mostly theoretical, historical and aesthetic, and our radio and audio production projects had been more literary and formally innovative. We wanted to invest our energies in something that was properly public facing, something capable of having a social impact.

At that moment, the news media buzzed with stories about an adolescent mental health crisis: referrals to children's mental health services had tripled; major depressive episodes among young people were spiking; reported incidents of anxiety, eating disorders and self-harm were all rising fast; and the NHS estimated that as many as 1 in 6 children had a probable mental health disorder. More and more research coming out at the time suggested correlations (if not outright causalities) between these mental health issues and children's media diets. This was not an abstract problem for us – not long before this, my own early-teen aged son had suffered a significant bout of obsessive compulsive disorder coupled with problematic online gaming and severe school stress. Lance and Tim also had their own experiences of adolescent mental health issues in their families. This hit close to home.

Some months earlier, Theresa May's government had issued its own green paper on the problem, *Transforming Children and Young People's Mental Health Provision*. But it made no proposals for new funding and seemed little more than an administrative exercise in rearranging the deck chairs on the *Titanic*. We decided this was an intervention we could make: we could use our networks, skills and expertise in podcasting, digital media, storytelling and comics to try to take a small bite out of this crisis.

Hoping to ground what we were about to do in the most current science, we first reached out to Professor Robin Banerjee, the Head of Psychology at the University of Sussex and Director of the Children's Relationships, Emotions and Social Skills (CRESS) Lab. For several years, the CRESS Lab had been at the forefront of research into children's deteriorating mental health, specifically how their media diets affect their values and how those values affect their mental well-being as young adults. We pored over their studies of the consumer culture ideals of materialism and appearance, how those ideals often relate to perceived improvements in image and status, and how striving after them often has negative implications for long-term mental health (particularly when compared to striving after connections with others). This had huge (and likely very funny) dramatic potential. Also, Robin and the CRESS Lab's extensive work into the well-being and the resilience effects of kindness and pro-social behaviours, particularly modelled in narratives, seemed a perfect foundation for an engaging children's media project intending to have a positive mental health impact. After several meetings with Robin (informally known as the 'Professor of Kindness'), with other contributors to the CRESS Lab, and much study of their years' of output, we distilled some key ideas into a departure document for the development of a kids' sci-fi adventure drama podcast/transmedia project we dubbed *The Rez* (slang for 'resilience').

When the funding was in place, we brought Hannah Berry (a recent UK Comics Laureate with experience in mental health comics) on board to lead a diverse team of writers that included Patrice Aggs, Simon Jowett, Rachael Smith, Halima Hassan and Abbigayle Bircham. At our writers' rooms, we refined our fictional future utopia in which consumption, competitive (and pointless) point-scoring and validation from others were everyone's focus, and in which things like kindness and authentic friendship had been largely forgotten. We further developed our two main characters: Preen, a mega-influencer whose fall from stardom prompts a re-assessment of his priorities, and Sav, a geeky outcast more concerned with finding her missing Gran than with likes, followers and 'chieves'.

We wanted to validate the knowledge and experience of young people today and include

*Part of **The Rez**'s teaching resources*

them as much as possible in the production process. So co-creation workshops were arranged with youth theatre companies and with schools, and a device was embedded in the story to allow young people's voices and ideas to be heard in the podcast: an ancient hacked phone that allows our heroes in the future to reach back to the 'Pastlings' (the real kids of the 2020s) to ask for help and advice about things like real friendship, repairing relationships after a fight, things to do in nature, bullying, dealing with isolation, recognizing stressors and the importance of withdrawing to recharge.

In 2020, as we were preparing to record our first season, the Covid-19 pandemic hit. This dramatically increased the stress on kids, and while it threatened to derail our production it also made the need for a project like *The Rez* even more clear to us. We pressed ahead and figured out the best way to record remotely so we could deliver the experience to young people in need of both high-quality entertainment during lockdown and resilience resources to confront the emotional challenges of the moment. In the end, *The Rez* became not simply something to supply young people with the emotional and social skills to ease a transition from primary school to secondary school, but a project that helps equip them with resiliency tools to deal with a range of traumatic events (large and small) that they might face while growing up. And while we've been pleased to document its wellbeing impacts through quantitative and qualitative research across 25 episodes, two comics and a host of PSHE-Association-accredited teaching resources, we've been equally pleased to clock its public success more broadly. *The Rez* has cracked the Top 20 charts in the US and the UK, has been recognized with numerous industry awards (including a Webby in 2022 and an ARIA in 2023), and has surpassed 400,000 downloads. We like to think it's as fun and funny as it is valuable and important. And it's led us to launch Rezilience Ltd, a company specializing in high-distribution, high-impact, audio-centric multimedia projects across a range of educational and wellbeing areas.

For others looking to undertake similar high-impact children's media project, the two *Rez* takeaways we'd offer are: 1) Getting real input from your audience at every stage of development, production and follow-up (through co-creation workshops, narrative devices to include actual voices, focus groups, etc) is indispensable in getting tone and language right, and refining messaging in content and outreach; and 2) today projects like this need integrated educational materials and a schools outreach plan to rise above the noise in the world of children's media.

CONNECTING BRANDS
WITH KIDS AND FAMILIES
SINCE 1999

RESEARCH
Full service agency and Kids Trends data

METAVERSE
We create award winning Roblox and Fortnite experiences

APPS & EDTECH
Our games are played by millions of kids and families

Dubit.io

hello@dubit.io

The Future Of Broadcast Media
According To Kids

Dr Eleanor Dare and **Dr Dylan Yamada-Rice**, Co-founders X||dinary Stories

We were commissioned by the University of York's XR Stories to explore what kids want from future broadcast media. Here, we focus on the methodology used and how this in turn raised questions about changing workflows in media production, where children could be included within these, and ethical issues for the media industry to consider further.

Using emerging technologies to allow children to share ideas about the future of broadcast media

The project was framed within the decline of children watching linear TV and the planned closure of traditional broadcasting of CBBC in 2025/6. In relation to this, we sought to understand how children aged 7–11 years old think brands might transition from TV to online digital, virtual or augmented spaces. To do this, we created a research methodology based around a series of public engagement workshops, where participants were offered opportunities to explore their ideas on the future of broadcast media in relation to a range of emerging technologies, such as photogrammetry, virtual reality (VR), augmented reality (AR) and proto-metaverse platforms (i.e. *Roblox*). Participants were asked to practically engage with these technologies and explore what they might mean for the future of broadcast content produced for child-audiences.

This was instigated through a series of practical prompts based on the heritage-brand *The Beano*, which were given to children during the public engagement workshops.

The long history of *The Beano* made it an interesting choice as the format of the stories has changed over time in relation to different platforms, e.g. comics, animation, and apps, which in turn has altered their connection to the audience. Following on from this, children were asked to explore how they thought other kids might engage with future *Beano* stories made with, or disseminated by, emerging technologies.

The prompts that were given to workshop participants included a range of *Beano* comics and figures which they were asked to use as inspiration to create characters and storyworld assets from Play-Doh, LEGO or cardboard that they wished to form part of interactive and/or immersive digital/virtual worlds.

The children's creations were scanned using a photogrammetry app to illustrate a simple way of producing 3D assets for virtual and digital spaces. Children who consented to take part in the research were informally interviewed about what they had created and why, in order to collect dialogue on their decision-making processes. Introducing children to photogrammetry and emerging technologies was also seen as offering them insight into new tools for storytelling that could form part of future broadcast media.

New workflows and ethical considerations

The outputs from the workshops gave us characters and story world assets, which we went on to explore in relation to creating immersive and interactive spaces by developing an AR app, *Roblox* game and two VR apps for both high- and low-end headsets, mindful that cardboard VR headsets cost about £5, and Oculus Quests cost from between £300 to £400. To make the AR and VR apps we rigged and animated some of the children's scanned 3D models and placed them within digital environments. These settings echoed the themes we saw in children's drawings. In the VR and AR experiences the animated characters danced with each other and, in response, we observed some children dancing with the animated models, often reaching out with their hands as if they could touch the digital objects/characters.

Children did not seem to notice much difference between the expensive VR system and the cheaper, less sophisticated one. None of the children made any comments about the image quality or the kind of 'immersive' characteristics manufacturers might emphasise.

In response to the apps, some children made comments about their own experiences using 3D modelling technology, games and platforms such as *Blender*, *Minecraft*, *Pokemon Go*, and *Roblox*. Children who used those technologies articulated firm opinions – that making games and characters themselves was the future of television and wider entertainment.

This was further expressed in relation to the *Roblox* game, where we were able to upload the digital assets of their physical models into the game-world. This allowed children to question this aesthetic in relation to the ones offered to them by adult designers and developers.

Further, the AR seemed anecdotally less engaging for children then the photogrammetry process, perhaps pointing to a kind of 'Ikea Effect' (the premise that people value things more or feel psychologically 'boosted' if they've made or partially made something themselves) in which children enjoy a workflow from analogue model creation to scanning an object into a 3D mesh, a process of transformation, echoing our research interest in the ways in which images and materials and our relationships with them can provide a fluid and constantly changing experience.

We experimented with using workshop outcomes such as the one used in the image below, with machine learning software to explore how children, designers of children's future broadcast media and machine learning might collaborate in the future. In this way, emerging software such as RunwayML (a machine learning platform for artists and designers) can be seen to combine with technologies, children and us as artists and researchers as a further extension to the complex assemblage of media production and audienceship.

Throughout this research project we have experimented with new and emerging digital-analogue workflows, including machine learnt processes of animation via interpolation in RunwayML, text to 3D model algorithms, such as *Mirage*, *Deforum* and *Stable Dream Fusion*, *MonsterMesh*, a beta sketch-based tool for drawing and animating 3D meshes online that has enabled an effective transit from analogue to digital 3D models for VR and AR. We also used Stable Diffusion (a machine learning image synthesis application) in industry standard software such as Unity and Blender, which further supported an efficient and materially different process of asset development, one which has the potential to make games and digital storytelling much more accessible to children and adults. But there are also very serious ethical issues entangled with machine learning.

Deploying machine learning in children's media raises many ethical issues, relating to the extraction of natural resources required to power huge datasets, the exploitation of 'Ghost' (Gray et al, 2019) workers and the underlying logic of machine learning which currently replicates some problematic categorisations, often racialised or reinforcing gender stereotypes. But there are also issues of copyright as well as representation, with machine learning models often not crediting the artists from whom images are derived. Using new media workflows ethically, with and for children (such is shown in the final image below that illustrates various AI generated images made from a child's Play-Doh model), necessitates an understanding of technical procedures but also a non-trivial grasp of their complex social and economic contexts. Future broadcast media will require nuanced reframing of concepts such as digital and media literacy and an understanding of data and media infrastructures.

Considerations for education, research and broadcasters

Education:

- Seek ways to bring analogue making into STEM and STEAM education to scaffold learning and allow children with less access to tech/internet to explore in their out-of-school lives.
- Seek ways to bring analogue making into digital making to produce a broader range of creativity.
- Develop media literacy that teaches children ethics connected to emerging technologies and AI.

Research:

- Push for research to be co-produced with children rather than relying on big data scraped off the back of devices they are using.
- Consider the role of children within a framework that includes adult developers of future broadcasting.
- Consider if the 5Rights framework needs to be extended to include emerging technologies.

Broadcasters:

- Consider how the narratives of stories relate to modes and materials.
- Consider the role of children in the design and development process.
- Consider using the Playful by Design cards as part of the development process.

References

Suri, S. and Gray, M. L. (2019). *Ghost Work: How to Stop Silicon Valley from Building a New Global Underclass*. Harper Business.

Untold Stories: Young Women's Perspectives Of The Future Of Public Service Broadcasting

Dr Becky Parry, Author and Researcher

The aim of *Untold Stories* was to gain an insight into the perspectives of young women aged 14–25 in Yorkshire, about the future of public service broadcasting (PSB). The BBC centenary provided a timely context, enabling young women to engage with relevant research and develop their own perspectives about the future role and responsibility of those making and sharing media for young audiences. Funded by XR Stories and the Arts and Humanities Research Council (AHRC), the project also enabled young women to access new immersive content and experiment with 360 sound and film production.

The role and history of PSB is not part of the school curriculum, so it was important to build the young women's awareness of models of broadcasting and of the concept of public service and the possibilities of newer technologies. In introducing these topics, we aimed to enable the participants to develop and share their own perspectives about the value of a 'public service' approach to the making and sharing of media. We used the idea of 'untold stories' to encourage young women to imagine themselves in the role of public service broadcasters with a responsibility to be the storytellers of the future.

Much research about children and young people in relation to media focuses on their engagement with a particular media form, such as videogames and, specifically a form such as *Minecraft*, as in my own research for example (Parry and Scott, 2019). Research also often positions young people as audiences or consumers of media, even where it acknowledges that media content provides opportunities for them to play and learn. Our aim was to enable the young women we worked with to take a more holistic perspective, considering the broader needs and rights of young people, particularly in relation to gender and childhood.

We took an arts-based (Parry, 2015), co-production and co-curation approach, involving Chol Arts, a Yorkshire based women-led theatre arts company that specialises in co-production and participatory arts, Lauren O'Donoghue, Jake Parry and Jon Harrison who led on digital storytelling, Meg Wellington-Barratt who led on photography, and Hadrian Cawthorne who facilitated the creation of a 360 digital exhibition in Mozilla Hubs. Working in this way enabled us to introduce research and develop shared responses, through a collaborative, creative process. Activities included a visit to Broadcast 100 exhibitions at the National Museum of Science and Media, meeting curators and hearing about the process of curation. A wide choice of further activities included creative writing and the production of interactive stories using (the open source storytelling tool) Twine, 360 film production, stop-motion animation and photography.

It was pivotal to the project to incorporate the perspectives of diverse young people with different gender identities and to be inclusive in relation to neurodiverse young people and those with disabilities. We were also interested in the perspectives of young women in Yorkshire in particular, as it is the region served by the funder XR Stories. We therefore identified a college with multiple sites for 16–25 year olds, Pinc College in Bradford, Halifax and Leeds, and a school in Sheffield, King Edward VII (KES), where we worked with 14–15 year old photography students. Both institutions serve areas of economic disadvantage and ethnically diverse communities and are non-selective state education providers. In total we worked with 32 young people and 12 teaching staff intensively and also presented their work in an exhibition to a further 200 students and museum visitors via the Cholovan pop-up exhibition and an online digital exhibition.

Insights from the project

Young women are media producers

The young women we worked with were media producers as well as consumers and they shared multiple ideas for new children's television programmes. Here we use the term producer to describe creative activity such as drawing,

filmmaking, music production that the young people were engaged in. These creative activities enabled the young women to pursue special interests and be part of a wider fan or collective culture. For example, one member of the group from Pinc College was a fan of the virtual idol 'vocaloid' Hatsune Miku who was a regular feature of her artwork.

Children's media is significant to childhood

The young women we worked with expressed great nostalgia for favoured media content from their childhoods, especially television programmes – although they often did not know who made the programmes or who broadcast or streamed them. Favourite content was often described as influential and important to their identities and linked to key childhood relationships.

Public service broadcasting for children is needed

The terms broadcasting and public service broadcasting were not familiar to them, but the young women had a strong commitment to children's television and felt that it should be a priority for funding.

New representations of girls

Some of the young women had strong feelings about the way media represented girls and women, and this was especially evident in their photographs of objects where they deconstructed childhood dolls. The need for diverse gender representation and representation of young people from the north and those with disabilities and neurodiversity in children's television was seen as important for the future. For example, one young woman loved *Bluey* in particular and created a set of LGBTQ+ characters or versions of *Bluey*, expressing her belief that media for children need to be inclusive and not afraid to deal with challenging ideas, such as miscarriage.

Incidental representation of diversity

In one of the activities there was an interesting discussion about incidental representation of characters who didn't fit gender or sexuality norms. For example, one young woman described the way *Adventure Time* had LGBTQ+ characters, but the story wasn't about their sexuality, it was just inherent to the fictional world and accepted as 'no big deal'. A similar point was made by one of the Pinc College group where several of the young people were either nonbinary or trans. They were keen for this to be accepted and wanted to see media representations where characters with different gender identities were included without this being the main feature of the storyline.

Youth media: on the cusp

The stories the young people created highlighted the way in which they are on the cusp of adulthood, whilst still interested in and nostalgic about childhood media favourites. Although many of them talked about reading youth fiction, mentioning favourite authors such as Malorie Blackman, there were few mentions of any favourite youth films, television programmes or games. That is to say, they recalled their childhood experiences or discussed their adult viewing and media engagement, but specialist youth media did not feature. This was also reflected in the Twine stories created by the Pinc College students, which were either for young children (a magic garden, rabbits and *Bluey*) or adult (dystopian, horror, thriller, *Family Guy*). Young women, on the cusp of adulthood and adult media, appeared to be interested in more complex media experiences, exploring existential themes, with diverse gender identities and humour, but they also seemed to be under served by existing youth media content.

Media careers: being the storytellers

Although women are employed in the screen industries, there are still comparatively few who are the lead writer or director of television drama,

Untold Stories workshops

film or games (Milner and Gregory, 2022). Only one of the young women we worked with explicitly expressed a desire to work in the media industry and she was a neurodiverse young woman, of South Asian descent with disabilities. This young woman expressed an interest in being a film director and she enjoyed creating a stop-motion animation as part of the project. However, her knowledge of potential pathways to this career route were limited and it is evident that any training schemes available to her would need to be able to remove barriers that would limit her participation. Interestingly, after the end of the project we have fielded quite a few requests for further information about media careers from parents, teachers and young people and especially about those linked to uses of newer, immersive technologies and interactive tools, indicating the value of 'taster' activities in terms of raising awareness of career possibilities.

New tools: new affordances

Students and teachers responded very positively to the introduction of new tools such as Twine for creating interactive stories and 360 microphones and cameras for creating new sound and moving image designs. Twine especially was seen as a valuable tool for enabling branching narrative storytelling and giving young people further agency in their storytelling. Staff all undertook professional development during the project, in order to be able to use this tool in the future independently. Most of the group enjoyed engaging with

360 content and creating a 360 film, though some were concerned about motion sickness and found the headsets uncomfortable. The neurodiverse students especially valued the way VR content can be relaxing and saw potential for new content that transports others to calm or non-threatening spaces. There was a clear role for artists and creative practitioners to introduce new digital tools in the context of education as a means of increasing access to new forms of creative media production.

Broadcasting futures

The concept of public service, in relation to media broadcasting, usefully highlighted the responsibility of mass media organisations to prioritise children and young people and tackle inequity. Insights from the project demonstrate the need to ensure that the rights of young women are a priority for those leading innovation in the development of new forms of media production and streaming and broadcasting, in order to ensure that there are diverse and rich representations of young women in the future. Young women, aged 14–25, also need to have more opportunities to represent themselves in order to avoid subjugation and the dominance of stereotypes (Aley and Hahn, 2020). This must also be a priority in relation to skill sector development and innovation in relation to the production of media content if we are to avoid duplication of inequity in terms of both representation and work force composition.

Recommendations

We told the young women and their advocates that we would be sharing their perspectives with broadcasters, funders and researchers. Their recommendations are as follows:

- Children's media content is formative, especially in terms of gender identity and therefore continues to be important in later life. Young women and girls need specialist content made for their age group (just as they need youth fiction in the form of books.)

- Young women (aged 14–25) should be seen as media producers, as well as consumers and they should be given opportunities to engage with new (and older) technologies, in order to develop their understandings of what creative processes they make possible.

- Neurodiversity, gender, LQBTQ+ identities and places in the north should be more frequently represented in the media and accepted (not problematised), including the use of incidental representation.

- Young women's knowledge and special interest in media and uses of digital technology need to be recognised in education more, especially in terms of skills development and progression opportunities.

- Barriers linked to gender that inhibit careers in the media industries need to be better understood and challenged, especially regarding intersectional disadvantage, in the context of apprenticeships, skills development schemes and traineeships designed to tackle inequity.

You can find the full exhibition in Mozilla Hubs:
https://hubs.mozilla.com/NbouHCC/untold-stories

Participant's Twine Stories:
https://laurenodonoghue.neocities.org/pinc23/untoldstoriesv1

References

Aley, M. and Hahn, L. (2020). The powerful male hero: A content analysis of gender representation in posters for children's animated movies. In: *Sex Roles*, 83(7–8).

Milner, S. and Gregory, A. (2022). Time for a change: women, work, and gender equality in TV production. In: *Media, Culture and Society*, 44(2).

Parry, B. (2015). Arts-based approaches to research with children: Living with mess. In: *Visual Methods with Children and Young People: Academics and Visual Industries in Dialogue*. Palgrave Macmillan.

Parry, B. and Scott, F. (2019). Researching children's play and identity in the digital age: A holistic approach. In: *The Routledge Handbook of Digital Literacies in Early Childhood*. Routledge.

Video Killed The Linear Star

Rachel Bardill, Senior Vice President, Marketing, The Insights Family and **Stavros Triseliotis**, Head Industry Analyst, The Insights Family

On a typical day, the average kid aged 6–12 in the UK spends 77 minutes watching TV shows. But where they have been watching and what they have been consuming has changed beyond recognition. YouTube has stolen the charge on grabbing kids' attention and keeping that attention on their platform, ensuring they spend more and more time feasting on video content of any kind – whatever the quality, length, subject matter and volume. This has had a huge impact on the kids media industry not only with the kind of content that gets commissioned, but with production values, genre and distribution methods too. It is an incredibly challenging landscape to commission against. It is an unsettling time to produce video content within. It is certainly confusing to understand where to put and how to amplify your content.

This article will investigate the widely accepted fact that linear television has largely been displaced by video on demand (VOD), and specifically YouTube. Using quantitative data from The Insights Family's Kids Insights and Parents Insights portals, we will discuss the implications of this phenomenon on the distribution of content that caters for young audiences. The data used reflects the opinions of two UK-based panels; 1,200 boys and girls aged 6–12 and 1,200 parents (both female and male) of boys and girls aged 6–12 surveyed during Jan–Mar 2023. All data collected, analysed and presented in this article is quantitative.

Bolstered by consumers' exposure to video content, the global content marketing industry revenue is expected to reach US$107 billion by 2026, according to data compiled by Statista. Within family ecosystems, content consumption constitutes the single most popular activity, which often serves as a pastime; however, it ends up becoming a big part of how parents spend time with their kids. 85% of British families with 6–12 year olds say they watch YouTube as a family activity (34% of 100% watch daily), while 95% say they watch TV (60% of 100% watch daily). It is, therefore, not a surprise that on-demand constitutes a significant part (if not the most significant) of today's IP. Indicative of this is the fact that nearly 2 in 5 (37%) of 6–12s surveyed said they have interacted with their favourite characters on YouTube, or a streaming platform, compared to 33% who played a game and 26% who bought a toy. On the other hand, linear TV (a platform that not that long ago was kids' one and only watching option) is preferred by 1 in 5.

While this demonstrates the effectiveness of VOD platforms as touchpoints to engage with kids, it also highlights the extent to which content consumption is increasingly shifting away from linear mediums and towards on-demand platforms. Giving further credence to this notion, Kids Insights data on watching frequency clearly shows that across the past five years, the gap between linear TV and YouTube has steadily become wider (see chart). Today, 6–12s are more than five times more likely to prefer watching YouTube (54%) than linear TV (9.6%). An additional 34% prefer Netflix and 2.9% mostly watch Amazon Prime Video. Could linear TV ever recover from the cannibalisation it has been experiencing or is it time to re-imagine linear to fit a different need of kids today?

It is evident that kids spend more time watching YouTube than linear television. Could this come down to device access and device functionalities? Kids Insights data suggests that amongst 6–9s, TV devices are almost exclusively used for watching episodes (66%) and clips (34%). Admittedly, portable devices allow higher

flexibility, with their primary purpose varying from user to user. For example, popular uses of tablet devices amongst the same demographic include watching episodes or clips, gaming, listening to music, watching tutorials, reading, doing homework and chatting (19%–41%). As much as TV devices have evolved into smart entertainment systems, the ways in which a TV mounted on a wall can be used cannot compare to how portable devices are used.

Additionally, portable devices allow for quick navigation across platforms and apps, enabling the user to enjoy an IP's ecosystem storytelling experience to its full extent. For example, beyond their favourite show (or clips of it) on YouTube, kids can interact with bonus content or user-generated content, including reaction videos or reviews. Compared to linear TV, YouTube is an entire content universe where IP territory is being expanded through its fans. Therefore, one aspect making linear TV less popular with kids compared to YouTube is how isolated a space it is.

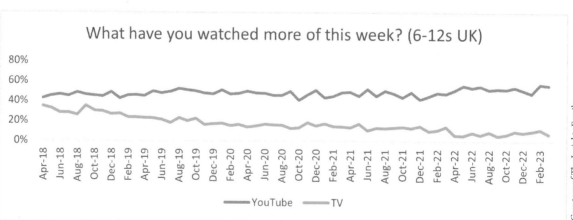

The gap between linear TV and YouTube watching frequency has steadily increased

A growing number of broadcasters recognise the need for a digitised and interconnected future not only for on-demand content but also for linear and curated content libraries. Sky with Sky Kids is the latest broadcaster to introduce an app-supported linear channel, launched in February. It may be a well-known fact, but detaching linear programming from TV devices enclosed within a single space, like a living room, is a challenge broadcasters still need to address more effectively.

When asked about how they chose their favourite platform, kids who prefer YouTube were more likely to value the personalised experience that it offers (+40%) and the wide variety of watching options (+78%). On the other hand, kids who prefer watching TV are more likely to do so due to their favourite TV shows being broadcast that way (+6%), which may suggest that linear programming is effective in cultivating loyalty. Furthermore, we see that parental approval plays a significant role in kids' choice of favourite platform, with kids who prefer watching TV being more likely to do so because their parents allow them to watch it (+40% compared to kids who prefer YouTube). In line with this, Parents Insights data shows that parents are more comfortable allowing their children to watch TV without approval, than YouTube (51% vs 34%).

Within a curated video content library that is reviewed, approved and primarily designed for its target audience, parents feel a higher level of control that their children will only be exposed to age-appropriate messages. But with 60% of kids having access to a mobile phone and 78% to a tablet device, can we really set a limit to the type of content kids will discover and grow fond of?

As discussed, there are certain areas where linear programming outperforms the on-demand format, including obtaining parents' blessings and cultivating loyalty. Furthermore, an interesting observation we have made with regards to advertising salience (a key performance indicator (KPI) that measures how well consumers recognise a brand) is that although YouTube is significantly more popular than TV, adverts on YouTube (23%) are not nearly as favoured compared to those on TV (39%). This may suggest that linear TV as a medium is capable of capturing kids' full, undivided attention, whereas YouTube ads (and possibly content) are likely to be watched passively.

Based on the above, the linear programming format's survival lies in its ability to evolve alongside its audience's expectations and finding a way to satisfy a variety of need states in the different ages of children. For instance, 3–6 year old children still absolutely enjoy sitting back and being served TV shows, at different times of the day. Older children need downtime and relaxation after school. Besides undergoing radical changes with regards to its delivery channels, linear programming should tap into its users' needs, which may come from how theme focused linear libraries are. Could this imply the need for the creation of personalised channels under the same network, which cater to niche audiences?

Furthermore, a significant aspect that, arguably, linear programming falls short of is user-generated content. Consumer Technology Association's report *Tech Enabling User Generated Content to Flourish* (2022) states that 39% of content consumed weekly is user-generated. Given the ease of content

creation and how important a feature creation is becoming for social media apps, user-generated content is only going to grow, which means that in order to resonate with modern kids, broadcast content professionals need to consider how to accommodate co-creation and interaction for the simple reason that their content needs to be relatable.

To say that linear TV has remained stagnant would be unfair; the last decade has seen many linear channels going online while linear TV advertising has become more sophisticated. However, with VOD being one of the main disruptive innovations of the past two decades, causing significant shifts in watching habits, in its current format linear TV does not address the habits and expectations of the modern user and will not resonate with future generations.

Children's Content In A Changing Commissioning And Distribution Landscape

Dr Cyrine Amor, Senior Analyst, Ampere Analysis

The tail end of the Covid-19 pandemic saw a flurry of activity in the overall content commissioning market, with investments by leading broadcasters and streamers reaching an all-time high. But as we emerge from this period, there has been a notable slowdown in commissioning activity since the second half of 2022, reflecting the maturity and saturation of the VOD (video on demand) market. Increased pressure within the industry to translate content investments into more sustained and sustainable revenue streams has been exacerbated by the current economic downturn.

The children's content market, given this, continues to undergo a number of changes. Content consumption patterns have changed, shifting away from linear modes of consumption to on-demand platforms. More children's content is available to consumers than ever before, and across a wider array of providers. At the same time, however, we're seeing reduced commissioning of new content in the market. This has been particularly tangible in the subscription video on demand (SVOD) led US market where major studio groups have made large-scale cuts to original content investments over the last three quarters, impacting scripted children's content commissions – especially animated content – more than other genres. But now in Western Europe, where public service broadcasters (PSBs) play a far more significant role in supporting a relatively stable content output, commissions of new children's content have also started to decrease – albeit at a less alarming rate than in North America.

So how should content producers and distributors interpret and navigate this changing market? What strategies should they adopt in approaching different types of market players with their content to maximise its visibility, popularity – and ultimately – financial success? To address these questions, Ampere Analysis has triangulated data from its Consumer, Analytics and Commissioning services providing both historic context of the trends observed and new insights into children's content over the last year (up to April 2023).

Childrens commissions nearly halved in the US in 2022

In the US, the SVOD market has reached maturity, and platforms are battling not only to attract new subscribers through original programming, but increasingly to retain them and show a viable path towards profitability. While the volume of total new US TV commissions has decreased overall, children's content has suffered the biggest cutbacks: it fell by close to 50% in the year to end of Q1 2023 compared to the previous year; across 'all TV' shows, by comparison, the decline was 'only' 13%.

The majority of cuts to new children's content in the country stem from paid TV and streaming players backed by the major US studios. Viewership on paid TV kids' channels such as Disney Channel, Nickelodeon and Cartoon Network may be in precipitous decline, but crucially these audiences have not yet moved over en masse to their sister streaming services such as Disney+, Peacock and Paramount+.

Given this, further investment in new children's commissions from the studios is unlikely to pay off in the short-term. Studios instead can serve their dwindling linear audience through library titles: Ampere's data indicates a rapid rise in the repeat rates on these channels, particularly for flagship studio channels like Nick Junior, Boomerang and the Disney channels.

These trends are compounded by findings from Ampere's consumer surveys on attitudes towards the availability of children's content. Consumers are confused by the volume of content available and the panoply of platforms needed to access it – leaving them eager for greater aggregation in their point of access. Moreover, data from Ampere's consumer survey at the end of 2022 indicate that children's content is not a primary driver for subscription to streaming services, even amongst family households (with the exception of Disney+). Most SVOD platforms' family subscribers ranked access to children's content outside of the top five motivating factors for subscribing, behind price, access to movies, and sports content.

This goes some way to elucidating why cuts to children's original commissions in North America are higher than the decrease in commission volumes in other genres. Against the backdrop of a downward market trend and budgetary pressures for streaming services, the case for content expenditure on children's commissions becomes more difficult to make.

In Europe, linear commissions are down but title availability has doubled

In Western Europe, the situation is different. The SVOD market is less mature and there's still more scope for these US-owned platforms to grow their subscriber base. However, Ampere's latest consumer survey in Western Europe suggests that for streaming services, children's content catalogues are not a key factor for new customers here either.

At the same time, the volume of children's content available to European audiences across different distribution platforms is rising. Since 2019, children's TV content available in Western Europe's leading five markets (France, Germany, Italy, Spain and the UK) has more than doubled by number of titles, with close to 7000 distinct titles available across linear TV channels, broadcaster VOD (BVOD) services, advertiser-funded VOD (AVOD) and SVOD catalogues in 2022.

The volume of linear titles available in Europe continues to decline, with 30% fewer children's TV programmes on offer in 2022 than in 2021, as SVOD becomes the dominant distribution method in the region. Close to 4000 distinct titles were distributed on SVOD platforms in Europe's leading markets in 2022, while BVOD and – increasingly – AVOD are taking off in the region too.

Effective distribution strategies key to standing out in a crowded market

A higher number of titles being made available generates more opportunities for children's content producers and distributors, but also heightens the risk of content being lost in the crowd. With so many titles available across so many platforms, what distribution strategies are proving most effective for children's content to stand out?

Content popularity data has been drawn on to answer this question. Ampere tracks content popularity through a metric assigned to each title, which serves as a cross-platform proxy for title engagement. Its calculation is based on key data such as volume of interest, web traffic and box office income from major services such as Google, Wikipedia and IMDb, which is normalised to produce a score for how popular a title is by market or region.

What has emerged from this data is a clear trend across markets that content distributed across multiple platforms – be it several linear channels or SVOD platforms or a mix of SVOD, linear, AVOD or BVOD outlets – achieves a higher popularity score than platform-exclusive content.

For example, on average in the US, content available across three to four different platforms in 2022 scores approximately twice as well as content available exclusively on one platform – and this trend holds true across a number of markets, including in Western Europe. Children want to watch what their friends are watching, regardless of the platform it is available on. The more platforms it is available on, the more chance they have access to it, and the more chance their friends have access to it too.

Exclusivity remains a key tool for SVOD platforms to attract subscribers, as SVOD services can attract adult customers with one hit show, and then lure them to stay with the content library on offer. However, when it comes to children's content, the viewer is not the one holding the credit card. TV content consumption patterns also tend to differ when it comes to children, as they are more likely to watch the same programmes and episodes repeatedly, thus exclusivity and time sensitivity are less important factors. That means exclusivity in kids' content is less likely to generate the kind of engagement and popularity that more widely distributed children's programmes do.

For the most high-profile established kids' content brands, exclusivity can be successful in drawing subscribers to a platform and adding value to their catalogue. However, beyond the likes of *SpongeBob SquarePants* and *Paw Patrol*, children's titles in the medium popularity range are more likely to achieve a consistent level of popularity by regularly appearing on different platforms or channels. Such a strategy allows these titles to attract new viewers or re-ignite interest and engagement, whereas heavily marketed platform exclusives might peak in popularity as they launch on SVOD, but swiftly disappear from children's radar. That's particularly true for completely new shows and IP.

An assessment of the popularity of children's titles first launched in 2020 shows that platform-exclusive titles lost approximately half of their popularity score within their first three months, with the occasional peak thereafter as new seasons launched. By contrast, content distributed on multiple platforms initially achieved a lower popularity rating at launch, but had far greater longevity, maintaining a consistent level of popularity over time. Multi-platform shows get a popularity boost not only from new seasons being released, but also with each new licensing deal and appearance on a new platform, overall only losing a few points in popularity score on average after two years.

In the context of a rapidly changing content landscape, with fewer projects commissioned and increasing challenges around standing out among the seemingly endless volume of titles on offer, it is clear that new children's content is more likely to benefit long-term from a multi-platform distribution approach to gain better engagement and popularity levels.

Photo by Alexander Dummer on Unsplash

Video Games And Child Financial Harm

Dr David Zendle, Behavioural Data Scientist and Lecturer in Computer Science, University of York

The way that video games make money has changed. In order to understand the current risks that in-game spending poses to children and young consumers, it is first necessary to map the magnitude of this change.

A brief history of video game monetisation

If we rewound time to the late 1990s, or even the early 2000s, we would see an industry whose revenue was mostly built around the idea of selling individual video games to individual consumers as individual end products. This is the world of games that I grew up with, and it may also be the one that you grew up with: a video game was a tangible thing that you could buy (whether in physical form or via digital download). Once you had bought it, you could play it as much as you liked. The way that publishers tended to make money via this strategy was straightforward: they tried to produce their products as efficiently as possible and attempted to sell them to consumers for more money than they cost to produce. The essential idea was to make more money from sales than was spent during production.

However, as the industry quickly discovered, this 'games as a product' approach was extremely high risk. Millions of dollars could be spent during designing, developing, producing, and advertising a game. If this money was not recouped during a relatively narrow 'premiere window' surrounding the game's launch, then a promising young studio could suddenly find itself deeply in debt and with no easy sources of new revenue. This is a very similar monetisation strategy to classic Hollywood studios and, like with classic Hollywood studios, rates of sudden bankruptcy amongst video game development houses was high. The industry rationally began seeking a way to make smoother revenue from its consumers: the jagged nature of product-based monetisation was simply too high risk for many.

Games as sales platforms and revenue smoothing

Over the past 20 years, one approach to monetisation has emerged that solves this problem and is thought to effectively smooth revenue streams: treating games not as products, but as sales platforms. In the west, the emergence of this strategy is typically associated with the role-playing game *Oblivion*. *Oblivion* was a wonderful game: it was set in a detailed fantasy world that players immersed themselves in. They could pick herbs, cast spells, fight brigands, and ride around on their horse. Horses were a big deal in *Oblivion*: they provided one of the few means to rapidly traverse the game's massive world. Initially, *Oblivion* was monetised in a traditional 'game as a product' manner – we all handed over a set amount of money (typically around £50) to purchase a physical copy or digital download of the game. However, what the developers of *Oblivion* did next was unprecedented.

In 2006 they offered players the opportunity to pay a small amount of money (around £2) to purchase a new item: horse armour. Horses in *Oblivion* were never armoured and now the only way that players could get their beloved mount shod in unique, good-looking armour was by purchasing it with this real money transaction (not in-game gold). Players had never heard of someone doing this before and 'horse armour' quickly became a scandal that enveloped the gaming community. Why would they pay money for something that should have been incorporated into the game for free from the beginning? However, whilst voicing outrage, the community also bought this armour in droves and it quickly became one of the best-selling digital downloads on the Xbox's store. Before long, the publisher of *Oblivion* was selling all kinds of different in-game things via the same strategy.

This was the birth of games as sales platforms and the birth of a new kind of language to describe this phenomenon: the micro-transaction, in which individuals pay real money for a small amount of in-game content. Over the past 20 years, this strategy has grown exponentially in terms of its prevalence and profitability. By 2018, it was estimated that the *Candy Crush* franchise alone made more than $1bn per year through the sale of in-game products and services; today, the global revenue associated with games as sales platforms is conservatively measured in the hundreds of billions of dollars.

Consumer harm

The games industry is famous for relentless innovation and outstanding creativity. When applied to the creation of enjoyable experiences or ground-breaking works of art, this has had many positive and socially beneficial consequences: children can now learn how to program by playing *Minecraft*, connect with their peers in *Fortnite* and gain satisfying experiences of mastery in games as diverse as *League of Legends* and *Pokémon*.

However, when applied to the design of sales platforms, this same creativity and innovation has led to the potential for negative consequences. Perhaps the most prominent in this domain are loot boxes: items in video games that players spend real money on, but whose contents are unknown at the point of purchase. Similarities between loot boxes and gambling products have garnered controversy in recent years, with research showing that the people (including children and young people) who spend the most money on loot boxes are also the most likely to experience problems with gambling.

Beyond loot boxes the general transition of many video games from products to sales platforms has also led to significant concern regarding consumer harm. When we asked gamers whether they felt a game had coerced or exploited them into spending money, they rapidly named dozens of strategies they perceived were present in the products that they played.[1] These ranged from 'dark design patterns', in which players felt tricked into accidentally spending money, to situations in which they were forced to pay money to avoid negative consequences (such

---

[1] https://link.springer.com/article/10.1007/s10551-021-04970-6

Image by pch.vector on Freepik

as the loss of a treasured character or item), and further to so-called 'nerf cycles', in which expensive content that they previously had paid real money for was unexpectedly downgraded (or 'nerfed') so that they would have to buy more in-game content in order to remain competitive.

Prevalence and risk

Recent years have thus seen an explosion of news stories regarding financial harm in video games. Instances of gamers spending thousands, tens of thousands, or even hundreds of thousands of dollars in-game abound. Whether you are a parent trying to work out what games your children should play, or an executive attempting to understand which organisation you should partner with, it is crucial to understand how games make their money. After all, nobody wants their child to become immersed in a world which will eventually demand they spend thousands of dollars or fall behind their peers; and nobody in a leadership role wants to risk shackling their reputation to such an organisation either.

My research cluster has recently taken strides towards understanding this issue in the mobile gaming domain through massive-scale data analytics. We have analysed billions of dollars of transactions drawn from tens of millions of gamers and thousands of mobile games to estimate whether some games might lead to risks of financial harm. Our results are published in full in a peer reviewed academic journal.[2]

In essence, we discovered that many games on the market are gentle in their revenue streams: they are monetised by having each of their players spend only a few dollars every year. Indeed, in many games even the top 1% of spenders only spend ten or twenty dollars each. This is good news for people who want to get involved in the mobile gaming market: this sector is often characterised as predatory, but our research shows that this is far from being the case universally.

However, we also discovered that gentle revenue was not universally prevalent. Indeed, about 10% of the thousands of games that we looked at were monetised in a pattern that we termed *hyper-pareto*: they were making almost half of their revenue from just 1% of their spenders. These individuals often spent thousands of dollars each. Indeed, in some games, 1 in 100 individuals tended to spend more than $10,000 each. The most money spent by a single individual in our dataset ranged into the low seven figures.

These monetisation schemes present obvious risks to both parents and professionals working in children's media. Are there any good rules of thumb to identify such games? Unfortunately, there is no easy solution here. Our research showed that certain genres tended to have

[2] https://dl.acm.org/doi/full/10.1145/3582927

individuals spend more than others. The average simulated gambling game, for example, had its top 1% spend over $2,000. An average family-genre game had its top 1% spend $31. So, on average, a simulated gambling product presents a higher risk of financial harm than a family game. However, this rule was not universal. In some family games, top spenders put in thousands of dollars each, where in some simulated gambling products, even the top 1% only spent a few dollars each. We also found that age ratings were of little help in this domain. Games that were rated age 17+ did tend to have their top percentiles spend more money, but even amongst games rated age 4+ there were many examples where 1% of individuals spent thousands of dollars each.

In summary, monetisation within the video games industry is extremely diverse. In some games, top percentiles spend so much money that it may be financially damaging to them (including children). Often, parents are told that they must understand the games that their children are playing. When it comes to things like violence, sex and drugs, there are well-established descriptors that allow us to understand at a glance whether a game contains content that we may wish to steer clear of. It is easy to preach that, before partnering with a games company or allowing our children to engage with a game, we must first do our due diligence on the potential for harm within that game. However, when it comes to child financial harms, this is currently a difficult task. There are no labels or descriptors that let parents or other stakeholders identify or isolate the games outlined above.

I believe that this does the community a disservice. Such information should be transparently available in order to allow consumers to make informed decisions for themselves and their children. Should games companies disclose how much money individuals tend to spend in-game? Should games in which extreme spending occurs be labelled in a meaningful and interpretable way? I would answer 'yes' to each of these questions. When it comes to the potential for child financial harm, usable information is almost never available. This is a poor state of affairs.

The Dark Side Of Early Childhood Mobile Gaming

Dr Ana Oliveira, Assistant Professor, Lusófona University, CICANT and **Dr Carla Sousa**, Assistant Professor, Lusófona University, CICANT

Play has always been central in human development studies, especially in early childhood. And we're not just talking about recent research – foundational authors like Piaget and Vygotsky were all about play too. It's been a key player in understanding how we grow and learn. Playing allows children to discover the world around them, stimulates creativity and imagination, and offers a wide range of opportunities to practice and enhance language, communication, emotional and social skills. In our day and age, early childhood education is increasingly intertwined with digital media, both in schools and at home, with a particular emphasis being placed on the impact of mobile games and their influence on how children interact, play and learn (Morgade et al., 2020).

There is a certain duality associated with this relationship. While young children become increasingly engaged with mobile games, concerns regarding problem gaming have emerged. At the same time, there is wide scholarship focusing on the educational benefits that mobile gaming can present – well-designed games can enhance cognitive skills, digital competencies, media awareness, digital citizenship and creative skills. But understanding how mobile games can negatively influence young children is fundamental; so that parents, educators, caregivers, as well as policymakers, designers and producers can take proactive measures to mitigate these effects.

Some scholars, such as Zagal et al. (2013), have identified specific shady and unethical game design patterns, labeling them as 'dark'. These patterns can negatively impact players by manipulating them against their own best interests.

Recent studies by the Ofcom, EU Kids Online and the Pew Research Center warn that children are playing online games from a young age and consequently are perhaps exposed to dark patterns sooner. Therefore, it becomes increasingly relevant to researchers, practitioners, educators and also media producers to understand these dark patterns when they appear prevalent. But knowing which dark patterns are dominant and what strategies are used in online – and particularly mobile – games for young children is fundamental. This is the first step to taking proactive measures to ensure a deep reflection on game design ethics, the promotion of game literacies in early childhood, and a safe and positive gaming environment for young children.

What positive skills are children acquiring from online play?

On a more positive side, the benefits of online play for children to develop and enhance their digital literacy skills development are many and have been well studied. As those such as Sonia Livingstone and Danah Boyd have stressed, by engaging with digital platforms, websites and apps children become familiar with different interfaces, learning to navigate them in an effective manner, developing social interaction skills and using digital media in a creative and responsible way. Online games also frequently present challenges, puzzles and other activities that require strategic thinking, analytical reasoning and decision-making. By immersing in these experiences, children are prompted to analyse different situations, think critically, conceive effective strategies and adapt their approaches and solutions to different scenarios. Inherently, these challenges are closely related to the development of creativity and imagination. Online play nurtures creative skills, allowing children to explore and (self)express their ideas in a digital context, through experience, bringing creative visions to life, and promoting a sense of agency and empowering them to think outside the box.

How dark patterns are clouding children's play experience

As part of our research in to the use of dark strategies in children's mobile games, we conducted qualitative analysis of the five most popular free educational games for 0–5 year olds on the App Store in February 2023, focussing on four major categories of dark patterns:

- **Temporal dark patterns** involve tactics that manipulate players into spending more time playing the game. These tactics often employ deceptive or coercive means to keep children engaged. Examples include playing by appointment, where players are required to log in at specific times to receive rewards and daily rewards that incentivise continuous play. Additionally, advertisements are used to interrupt gameplay and prolong the time spent in the game.

- **Monetary dark patterns** employ deceptive tactics to pressure or coerce players, including young children, into spending money on the game. One common example is the 'pay to skip' feature, where players are offered the option to pay to bypass certain levels or challenges. Paywalls are another prominent dark pattern, restricting access to advanced features or content unless a payment is made. These tactics exploit children's limited understanding of money and can lead to unintended and potentially harmful financial consequences.

- **Social dark patterns** leverage a player's social connections with friends and family to generate benefits for the game. While our analysis did not find explicit examples of social manipulations in the games studied, it is important to note that these manipulations can have a significant impact on children's play experiences. Examples of social dark patterns include social pyramid schemes, where players are encouraged to invite others to join the game for rewards, and the fear of missing out (FOMO), which creates a sense of urgency to participate in the game to avoid feeling left out.

- **Psychological dark patterns** aim to manipulate players' decision-making processes and may not be in their best interest. These strategies exploit psychological vulnerabilities to influence player behavior. One example is the use of invested or endowed value, where players are encouraged to feel a sense of ownership or attachment to virtual items or progress in the game. Aesthetic manipulations, such as using visually appealing graphics or rewarding animations, are also employed to engage children emotionally and keep them invested in the game.

Among the different types of shady tactics used in the games we studied, only social manipulation was not found. However, the games included elements of manipulating time, money, and psychology to some extent. Visual tricks and strategies were common to all games and they were used to pressure young players into achieving all items or accessing all hidden features in the game. Paywalls were also a prominent dark pattern in four out of the five games and compelled children to pay to access certain advanced features. Furthermore, advertisements were present in all of the games.

Opportunities and risks?

Any distinction between positive and negative influences of mobile games in early childhood should balance the positive outcomes children acquire from online play, such as digital literacy, social interaction, critical thinking and creativity, while being cautious about the potential negative effects of dark patterns, including excessive screen time, financial exploitation and emotional manipulation.

Based on our findings, our suggestions to those that produce games and those that work with them, are that monetisation strategies should avoid the use of dark patterns, promoting a critical use of mobile games and also a positive learning and growing experience. Furthermore, the collective promotion of ethical game design should also prioritise the wellbeing of young children, offline play and shared gaming experiences.

References

Morgade, M., Aliagas, C., and Poveda, D. (2020). Reconceptualizing the home of digital childhood. In O. Erstad, R. Flewitt, B. Kümmerling-Meibauer, and I. S. Pereira (eds) *The Routledge Handbook of Digital Literacies in Early Childhood* (pp109–122). Routledge.

Zagal, J. P., Björk, S. and Lewis, C. (2013). Dark Patterns in the Design of Games. *Proceedings of Foundations of Digital Games 2013*.

Can **Same-Language Subtitles** Help Children to **Learn to Read?**

Dr Kathleen Rastle, Professor of Cognitive Psychology at Royal Holloway, University of London, **Dr Anastasiya Lopukhina**, Postdoctoral Research Fellow at Royal Holloway, University of London, and **Dr Walter van Heuven**, Associate Professor of Psychology at University of Nottingham

Learning to read is the most important milestone of a child's education. If children can't read, then they can't use reading to learn, putting them at a serious disadvantage in secondary school. The ability to read well is also a central requirement of accessing employment, social benefits, and public services as children move into adulthood. Yet, over 15% of children leave school with reading skills that are too poor to allow them to participate effectively in life.

Unlike learning to walk or talk, children aren't born with the capacity for reading. Instead, reading is a learned skill whose mastery requires around ten years of instruction, dedication, and practice.[1] There has been substantial investment in making sure that children receive optimal, evidence-based instruction in the first years of primary school. However, even with the highest-quality instruction, children will not become fluent readers without a great deal of reading practice. Unfortunately, surveys by the National Literacy Trust indicate that only around half of children enjoy reading, and less than one-third engage in daily reading outside of class.[2] Likewise, not all children have access to enjoyable, age-appropriate books to read at home.

A low-cost solution with potentially staggering returns

One innovative proposal is that children might be able to get valuable reading practice through *same language subtitles* (sometimes called captions) on streaming or television services. Campaign groups including *Turn on the Subtitles* and *CaptionsON* argue that turning on subtitles by default for children's media is a low-cost intervention with potentially staggering returns. Indeed, research by Ofcom suggests that children watch almost six hours of broadcast television (including catch-up) and over ten hours of paid-for on-demand content per week.[3] This degree of exposure equates to reading over 1000 pages per week for the average Year 4 child, according to the reading calculator available on the *CaptionsON* website.

These campaigns have attracted considerable attention in recent years from celebrities, media stakeholders, and governments. However, their claims are based on a relatively poor evidence base. We know that skilled, adult readers' attention is automatically drawn to subtitles and that many adults choose to use subtitles to aid understanding. There is also evidence suggesting that subtitles support comprehension in deaf and hard-of-hearing populations and in second language learners.[4] However, research on how subtitles might support children learning to read for the first time is sparse. Studies that have been undertaken to address this question have had small samples and suffer from poor design choices that make it difficult to draw strong conclusions. These studies have also tended to use older children as participants who already have some reading experience.

The notion that a child might learn to read or improve their reading just by watching television is an attractive one. However, there are good reasons to be sceptical of the claims being made. For one, we have virtually no understanding of the point in reading acquisition at which subtitles might be most useful. Do subtitles help from the very beginning of learning to read, or do children need to reach a certain level of reading proficiency before they devote attention to the subtitles? One could imagine that the youngest children or those with lowest reading proficiency ignore subtitles altogether. After all, to children who are not yet capable readers, the symbols of writing are just arbitrary lines, squiggles and dots. It seems more likely that subtitles benefit the development of *reading fluency* once children have already received some degree of instruction. However, it has long been known that effort is an important ingredient

of robust learning (for example, testing oneself on a solution as opposed to simply studying the solution). It may be that incidental exposure to subtitles whilst watching a television programme does not require sufficient effort to build the neural pathways required for reading. Finally, emerging research suggests that books use much richer vocabulary and more complex syntax than spoken language. We do not have a good understanding of the nature of language used in television and films, but we should not assume that it is the same as the language used in books.

Erik Schepers on flickr

Using eye-tracking to study children's reading of subtitles

The Nuffield Foundation recently awarded research funding to our team to study whether subtitles help children to learn to read. We plan two large-scale experiments with children in primary school using a technique called 'eye-tracking'. In each experiment, children will be placed in a chinrest to minimise head movement and asked to watch age-appropriate videos with or without subtitles (see Figure 1). Following a calibration procedure in which the eye-tracker locks on to the participant's pupil, we can detect precisely where on a screen the child is looking and how this changes millisecond by millisecond as they watch the video.

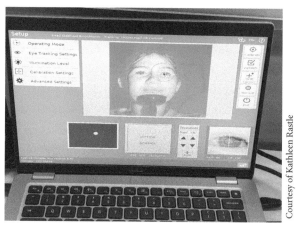

Courtesy of Kathleen Rastle

Figure 1. Experimental setup allowing us to probe how the eyes interrogate videos with or without subtitles.

We're then able to measure whether and how children are reading the subtitles in two ways. One approach is to measure how children deploy attention when watching subtitled and non-subtitled videos. To do this, we segment each frame of the video into regions of interest, and then generate *heatmaps* that reflect how long children spend looking at those different regions (see Figure 2). In general, we would expect children to allocate more attention to the subtitle region when there is a subtitle present, and when the subtitle is meaningful to them (because they have sufficient reading skill to understand it). In cases in which children devote attention to the subtitle region, we're then able to go further and measure how children engage with each word in the subtitle. We can measure whether the eyes land on a particular

word, how long they stay on each word, and whether the eyes go back to previous words. These analyses allow us to build up a picture of whether children are actually reading the subtitles (as opposed to just looking at them).

Courtesy of Kathleen Rastle

Figure 2. Heatmap showing eye fixations in a scene from a subtitled video. It is evident that attention is being allocated to the subtitle region.

Our planned experiments

Our first experiment asks to what extent children in primary school pay attention to and read subtitles. We will work with schools in southeast England to recruit around 30 children in each of the six year groups in primary school (Years 1 through 6). These children will watch a series of age-appropriate videos with and without subtitles. Our hypothesis is that engagement with the subtitles will increase as children get older and become more proficient readers. The youngest, least proficient readers may not pay much attention to the subtitles at all, while the oldest, most proficient readers may start to show the automatic attention to subtitles characteristic of adults. This experiment will help us to discover whether there is a sweet spot of age and reading proficiency at which subtitles may be most effective in supporting children learning to read.

Our second experiment is a randomised controlled trial investigating how subtitles exposure influences children's reading. We will select primary school children in the sweet spot identified in the first experiment, and ask them to document their viewing of broadcast television, catch-up, and paid-for on-demand content for a period of six weeks. Half of those children will be randomly allocated to the 'subtitles' group and asked to turn on television subtitles for that whole period, while the other half will be randomly allocated to a 'control' group asked not to use subtitles. We will assess both groups' reading before and after the six-week period, using both eye-tracking while children watch subtitled videos (as in our first experiment) and standard reading proficiency tests. If subtitles exposure supports children's reading, then the subtitles group should show greater improvement in their reading than the control group. This result would provide a compelling justification for a national intervention in which subtitles were switched on by default for children's programming. We will also use qualitative analyses to investigate children's experience with the subtitles, whether they've continued to use subtitles, and whether the subtitles have influenced their enjoyment of reading.

We hope that colleagues in the children's media space will share our enthusiasm for this project and will want to get involved. Every child has the right to learn to read well, and provided we observe a positive impact of subtitles in our experiments, then we have a chance to make a massive difference to the life chances of children in the UK and around the world.

Endnotes

[1] Castles, A., Rastle, K., and Nation, K. (2018). Ending the Reading Wars: Reading Acquisition from Novice to Expert. *Psychological Science in the Public Interest*, 19(1), 5–51.

[2] Clark, C. and Picton, I. (2021). *Children and young people's reading in 2021: Emerging insight into the impact of the pandemic on reading.* London: National Literacy Trust.

[3] Ofcom (2022). *Children and parents: Media use and attitudes report 2022.*

[4] Gernsbacher, M. A. (2015). Video Captions Benefit Everyone. *Policy Insights from the Behavioral and Brain Sciences*, 2(1), 195–202.

Rhyming, Repetition And Poetry Out Loud – Key For The Learning Brain

Prof Usha Goswami, Director of the Centre for Neuroscience in Education at the University of Cambridge

Here in Cambridge, we are running brain imaging projects with babies and young children to deepen our understanding of how the brain processes language – and to discover how dyslexia and oral developmental language disorders might begin. Our infant studies show that the brain uses rhythm to build a language system. Our speech modelling studies reveal that BabyTalk ('Parentese') exaggerates the rhythm structures in speech. Parents unconsciously produce rhythmic markers approximately twice a second when speaking in Parentese, placing great emphasis on stressed (louder) syllables. Most English nouns have a first syllable stress pattern, as in MUMM-y, DADD-y, BA-by. Language play with infants also foregrounds rhythm, as in 'knee bouncing' games like "Horsie Horsie don't you stop" and language repetition games like "Peek-a-Boo!". Making rhythms out loud – singing nursery rhymes, speaking poetry, marching to "The Grand Old Duke of York" and clapping out "Pat-a-Cake, Pat-a-Cake, Baker's Man" – is fundamentally important for the brains of toddlers as they learn language. Our research also shows that developmental dyslexia and oral developmental language disorders are associated with difficulties in processing rhythm patterns.

Our studies are designed to understand how a child's brain processes the speech signal acoustically, and what might be happening neurally. Acoustically, sound is conveyed to the brain as a pressure wave. When we speak, we are creating sound waves, moving energy through the air to the ear. The brain records these energy changes, which are speech rhythms. A good way of thinking about sound waves is by thinking about waves in the sea, continually moving and reaching the shore. There are some very dominant waves, like the waves the surfers catch, but there are also lots of other smaller waves, and it's the same in the speech signal. The brain cares about all these waves, large and small.

The brain catches this information about sound waves by electrical signalling: by using brain waves. You can think of brain signals as being like fireflies signalling on a dark night in a quiet forest. The fireflies are signalling at random and so is the listening brain in the absence of sound. But when a speech signal arrives, it is as though someone starts rhythmically banging a drum in the forest, and all the fireflies start signalling in time with the drumbeat. The fireflies are now signalling rhythmically, creating an electrical rhythm. In a similar way, the brain responds to the speech signal by making its electrical rhythms (brain waves) align with (or surf) the sound waves. There are lots of different acoustic rhythm patterns nested in the speech signal, which are created by the way in which our vocal tract works. Each brain network picks out their rhythmic tempo and responds in time. And all the brain networks are connected to each other in a signalling hierarchy, so that slower brain waves govern the response rate of faster brain waves. The brain's activity is like a nested cascade of different rhythms, with slower rhythms at the top. This enables a very complex representation of the sound signal that is human speech.

Rhythm is thus a hidden factor in how children learn and process speech. The exaggerated rhythms of BabyTalk and the metrical poems that are nursery rhymes play an essential role in language development. The acoustic timing of speech that is deliberately rhythmic depends on when the vowel is produced. If you deliberately repeat two words like "sweet" and "street" in a rhythm, the key to creating a regular rhythm is timing the pronunciation of "eet" in these words. In effect, you have to begin saying "street" earlier than "sweet", because "street" has more sounds before the vowel. The vowel is key to rhyming patterns in language – eat, seat, sweet, street. We can think of features like this as a kind of acoustic statistics. There are systematic sets of rhythmic statistics that are naturally embedded in the way that we speak, and even the pre-verbal baby's brain is learning these statistics. For babies, learning the sound structure of language is usually automatic and unconscious. The infant brain begins to learn these acoustic statistical patterns from hearing Parentese. The more language an infant hears in Parentese, the faster their language development. Nursery rhymes and other poems also exaggerate these acoustic statistics. Think of W.H. Auden's "This is the night mail, crossing the border, bringing the cheque and the postal order…". The internal rhythmic patterning of the words creates the rhythm of the train's motion, enhancing the imagery.

If you are listening to a foreign language that you cannot speak, you can still hear rhythmic patterns at different timescales. However, our studies show that infants who are at genetic risk for dyslexia do not experience efficient unconscious learning of rhythm statistics. Our research finds that infants at genetic risk for dyslexia already show difficulties in processing acoustic rhythm cues by 10 months. These rhythm cues help the brain waves to 'lock on' to the rhythms in speech, in essence to catch the critical peaks in the sound wave and thus surf it successfully. So already in infancy, the dyslexic brain is learning language differently. The dyslexic brain is 'in tune, but out of time'. These processing differences have important consequences for spoken language learning. One way to think about the neural basis of dyslexia is that acoustically the brain is always coming in either late or early. Some of the brain waves are not surfing the sound waves as accurately as in other children's brains.

To imagine what this means for speech processing, think about how difficult it can be to listen to a non-native speaker of English. This person may well have learned all the individual speech sounds (phonemes) correctly and may be saying them in the right order (the order in which they are written). However, they may still use the rhythm and stress patterning of their native language. If this stress patterning differs from English, as it frequently does, it can be very difficult to understand what is being said. We need listening experience to 'train our ears' to the persistent mis-timing of the rhythm structures of the English words. Speech rhythm (strong and weak syllable 'beats') is part of the hidden structural glue that makes individual speech sounds into recognisable words. It is this hidden glue that children with dyslexia find so difficult to hear. This does not mean that dyslexic children cannot speak and comprehend language successfully, as these children do not show obvious oral linguistic difficulties (although their difficulties are revealed in experimental tasks). But the children with dyslexia are learning language by relying on different acoustic cues to other children. This doesn't matter for speaking and being understood, but it does matter for interpreting written speech, that is learning to read. This is true in every world spelling system, not just spelling systems that use the alphabet.

Children with oral developmental language disorders also show difficulties in hearing and creating rhythm. These children were previously thought to have difficulties with syntax and grammar in language rather than with acoustic rhythm. They make obvious oral mistakes like "She comb her hair" and "Yesterday I fall down". However, detailed studies reveal that these children have very similar acoustic rhythm difficulties to children with dyslexia. They cannot really hear syllable stress patterns and they cannot hear rhythmic timing very well (e.g., when a pause occurs in speech, such as at the end of a syntactic phrase). They find it difficult to tap in time with a beat. Studies in French suggest that these syntactic problems decrease when the children listen to classical music just before performing a linguistic task. We don't yet understand why this is the case, but the formal rhythmic structure of the music seems to hold the key.

Our own research suggests that music therapies might be very effective for improving speech processing. Rhythm is more overt in music than in language. Coordinating musical rhythm with the 'syllable beats' of speech is the key, as rhythmic activities in the absence of language are not so effective. The music needs to provide a structure for the rhythmic patterns in the language. Singing to music is a natural way of achieving this. Interestingly, research with adults who have specific musical difficulties (amusia, or tone deafness) suggests that these adults are 'in time but out of tune'. Their brains are able to organise rhythm cues but not pitch cues. This is the mirror image of our research findings with children with dyslexia or developmental language disorder. Their brains cannot organise rhythm cues as effectively as other brains.

Because of the way that our brains work, it is really important to have fun with oral language rhythm patterns. Play clapping games like "Pat-a-cake" and clap the rhythms with your toddler, sing nursery rhymes like "Jack and Jill" together and use a bongo drum to beat out the syllable patterns, march along to "The Grand Old Duke of York" or bop to a rap song. Read rhythmic stories like *Room on the Broom* by Julia Donaldson or *Hairy Maclary* by Lynley Dodd. Learn poems by heart and say them together out loud, change the words to make it funny but keep the beat. Play skipping games to emphasise the underlying 'beat structure' of speech. All these activities should help the brain waves to surf the sound waves more accurately, and to come in on time.

Courtesy of Usha Goswami

Children's Audio: The Power Of A Journey Through Sound

Johnny Leagas, Children's Audio Consultant

I consider it a huge privilege to produce audio content for curious ears. I passionately believe in the power and influence audio has on the developmental stages of young children as they learn to listen and navigate the world in which they live. As such, I have specialised in (predominately preschool) children's audio and every series or piece of content I have commissioned or produced over the years has had the needs of little listeners at its heart.

Thoughtfully conceived and produced children's audio content can heighten children's curiosity and imagination, similar to how books and stories when read out loud or shared, transport children into other worlds, full of fun, magic and colour. Audio content has the ability to elevate the senses further, from just listening to actually 'feeling' emotions portrayed in poems, songs and stories.

That said, children's audio production is no easy task and replacing screentime and other visual stimulation with 'random' voices, music and sound effects filling the air out of nowhere, does come with considerable challenges.

In order to take children on an audio journey, it's vital that parents and caregivers introduce listening activities into family routines, to support the developmental research and benefits audio content offers. As a way to help whet children's audio appetites, I looked for inroads into their media consumption of popular brands and well-loved characters. This led to me developing and adapting children's animations to create many successful audio brand extensions. Harnessing children's (and their families') existing trust, love and relationship with these brands and characters helped to promote willing engagement, with a focus of listening to familiar voices leading them through stories and adventures, rather than watching them on screen.

In addition to branded content, original content plays an influential role, offering untold opportunities to engage, educate and entertain little ears.

Tone, language and performance play another vital role in children's audio production. None more so than when it comes to telling stories. In particular classic heritage stories, which are taught, shared and enjoyed by generation after generation, such as *Little Red Riding Hood*, *The Three Little Pigs* and *Goldilocks*, etc. Another rewarding and creative aspect of my role is the opportunity to work with some of the UK's most talented writers, developing and commissioning projects that breathe new life into such stories, keeping the morals and messaging whilst delivering surprising and contemporary twists. Anecdotally, this approach challenges the child's perceptions of the stories and offers alternative possibilities and opportunities for the characters and the stories they inhabit.

Another really popular and useful piece of audio ammunition to help encourage further engagement and a more concentrated listening experience, is to write and develop quizzes about stories. I have successfully taken this approach when working with licensed audio books such as *The Snail on the Whale* and other modern classics, and by doing so turned a passive listening experience into a more inclusive and interactive one.

Not surprisingly, poems and nursery rhymes are incredibly popular; children love repetition and as such these elements of content fast become family routine mainstays. That said, it's important to make sure we offer variety and so by rejuvenating familiar content such as nursery rhymes, it allows the opportunity to again build upon familiarity of spoken words and speech patterns, yet presenting the content in new and dynamic ways. A good example of this treatment is a musical series of nursery rhymes set against a variety of musical styles, tempos and rhythms, and performed by engaging and established vocal talent. These nursery rhymes were further enhanced by the performer and presenters actively speaking directly to the listening child. Shout outs, instructions and words of encouragement all help to promote a sense of inclusion and participation, which can be enjoyed solo or as part of group activities with friends and family. The same goes for other forms of songs and music genres. Music has the power to connect and inspire its audience.

Returning to my opening remark; my job is a huge privilege and I genuinely care about the potential and importance that audio content can have on the lives of children and their families. I am full of pride and admiration for my peers and creative colleagues who serve probably the most demanding and vulnerable of audiences. Thank you, and please let's continue to work so that we can encourage, challenge, inspire and entertain the next generation of audio consumers.

Returning To Work In Children's Media After Having Children

Emma Hyman, Creative Director, Tiny House Productions

Spoiler alert: it's harder than it should be!

I'm going to tell you my story and, whilst it's about me, I'm pretty sure it isn't unique in the industry.

I was a development producer with a decade worth of experience in the UK's best production companies when I left TV to have my first child. I was pretty burnt out by the freelancer lifestyle and was grateful for a break to be with my new baby to carve out my new identity as a mother. Over the first few years, I retrained as an antenatal teacher and had another child.

At this point I had no intention of coming back to TV. Why would I? I didn't want the long hours, the unpredictable contracts, the huge stress and to pay someone else most of my earnings to look after my children.

But as the years ticked along, I found a piece of me was missing. I wasn't Emma Hyman, 'sparky creative' anymore, I was just a mum and it wasn't fulfilling me in the way I needed.

After six years, I decided it was time to try and come back and this is where it started to get challenging. It was a sufficiently long enough time that I'd lost contact with much of my carefully stoked network. I eventually joined Media Parents who were incredibly helpful and plucked up the courage to go to a few networking events. They were terrifying but one of them was at a company that I'd worked at years before and they asked me to come back for a short contract.

So, I was back in the game – easy! Except that it wasn't. It was brutal! My once peers were now very senior. I wasn't up to speed and I'd softened over the years. Very quickly the tiny bit of confidence I had dissolved, my contract was being extended on a day by day basis, which made organising childcare impossible, and I came away from the experience crushed.

For several years after that, I searched for work but was too scared to look in the right places. I had another baby. My confidence was rock bottom. I went for job interviews where they didn't show up, I did little jobs where they forgot to pay me, and here's a truth: the worse you are treated, the worse you feel about yourself and you keep aiming lower and lower.

All the while, it was easy to forget that I had once had an amazing career, working with the best people in TV, with incredible training, on amazing shows, but as the years ticked by, that seemed to make no difference.

Then three things happened that changed my trajectory:

1. An old friend and colleague offered me a two week contract in adult TV out of the blue. After so long out of work – by now it was 10 years, I had a day to prove myself. I went into that job three days later with a list of 60 ideas! Needless to say, I did good and I stayed in that job for two years. I just needed a chance and I needed a soft landing to get myself up to speed with colleagues that knew what it's like to work and be a parent and know that these two things aren't mutually exclusive.

2. I plucked up the courage to go to CMC completely alone, which was one of the most terrifying things I've ever done and tried to re-build a network. I've never been so sweaty as I was in those Speed Meetings but they were a good reminder that I could do this!

3. And I re-found an old colleague who had recently semi-retired and the two of us started to meet to chat about new ideas. He believed in me and helped me to push the ideas forward. He loved my ideas and helped build my confidence and craft. My third child was 6 months old when I first thought of *The Baby Club*, and subsequently *The Toddler Club*. It was born out of a need I had and a life I was living. My experience led me to an idea that no one had thought about before. Would I have thought of that if I hadn't had time off? I doubt it.

Courtesy of Emma Hyman

The Baby Club *and* **The Toddler Club**'s
100ᵗʰ episode celebrations

So that's my story and here's what I've learned from it...

Here's why TV is not an attractive industry when you're a new parent:

- The hours are bad, the work is unpredictable and it's impossible to plan childcare.
- The freelance nature and fast staff turnaround means maintaining networks whilst you're on a career break is more challenging than other industries.
- The you're-only-as-good-as-your-last-job mentality: if that job was a long time ago, you start to become invisible (out of sight, out of mind!).
- Budgets and schedules are so tight that companies are understandably risk-averse to staff who have been out of the game.

Here's why we need women to return to work after having a baby:

- We KNOW the audience – so specific to children's media. You're literally in it, you know the audience better than anyone.

- We are losing a huge section of the experienced workforce. It takes years to develop knowledge.

- Yes, time out means you may be behind with the latest tech or the current commissioners but these can be learned quickly, unlike the skills developed over time.

- Time away doing other things gives a new perspective. I doubt I'd have thought of *The Baby Club* if I hadn't become an antenatal teacher or run baby groups myself.

- Time management – as any mum knows, if you have a window, you get stuff done, no mucking around!

- Work–life balance: there's no question, life comes first and that's good for everyone to remember. It makes us more compassionate and empathetic leaders and colleagues.

So what can we do about it?

- Someone gave me a chance: if you're an employer, actively go out of your way to give someone else a chance! We talk about diversity in the workforce, women returning to work are diverse and have relevant life experience.

- Support: if I look back at that first job I did after a long break, I know that I wasn't bad at the actual job, I just needed some help re-finding my feet. If I'd had a mentor, I'm fairly sure the outcomes would've been different.

- Flexible approach: it's been six years since I came back and I'm really hoping the industry has changed for the better. Covid has given us new ways of working and a greater ability to work flexibly. I hope the days of chaining staff to a desk until an arbitrary 6pm are a thing of the past and, if not, they really should be! Trust your workforce to do the job at the time that suits them best. Different ways of working: maybe it's time to think about job shares, especially for the female dominated world of Production Managers. If a job share works it's win win – happy team, plus double the brainpower!

It's taken a long while for me to appreciate that those years I took off to be with my children weren't wasted in terms of my career. No parent should return back to TV regretting, being embarrassed or feeling ashamed about stepping away from work to be with their children. And no parent should be put off returning to work because the industry isn't equipped to welcome them back.

THE INSIGHTS FAMILY®

RESEARCH · DATA · INSIGHTS

THAT CONNECT YOU WITH THE NEXT GENERATION

We provide the most comprehensive real-time market intelligence on kids, teens, parents, and families.

CHECK OUT OUR PORTAL
theinsightsfamily.com/login

DID YOU KNOW?

https://theinsightsfamily.com

52% of 6 -12s in the UK
enjoy watching comedy shows, making comedy the top genre across all platforms

41% of kids
aged 6-12 spend at least one hour watching TV on a typical school day

Kids aged 6-12s (UK)
76 % watch YouTube daily & 55% watch streaming daily & only 29% watch standard TV

Licensed TV show toy
purchases amongst kids & tweens in the UK has seen a year-on-year increase of +13%

INTRODUCING OUR BRAND MANAGEMENT PLAYBOOK 2023

go.theinsightsfamily.com/brand

"Mon The Weans!": A Brief Look At Children's TV In Scotland

Terri Langam, Head of Children's, Hello Halo Kids

When my soon to be 18 year old boys were little, their favourite TV shows were *The Dog Ate My Homework*, *Copycats* with Sam and Mark, *All Over the Place* and *Dennis the Menace and Gnasher*. All these shows were 'made in Scotland' and Scotland is still home to great children's TV.

I'm Head of Children's for Hello Halo Kids in Glasgow and we've been going since 2018. Our current shows include *Ranger Hamza's Eco Quest* with the fabulous wildlife presenter and camera operator Hamza Yassin (fresh from lifting the *Strictly* glitterball trophy); *Dog Squad*, our scripted live action series about real life assistance dogs; and *Get Set Galactic*, our preschool hands-on science gameshow, which we filmed in studio at BBC Pacific Quay, with their incredible in-house studio crew. All for CBeebies. We've got a fantastic team, all dedicated to making the most entertaining and diverse children's content we can.

Just down the road, BBC Studios Kids and Family Productions are based at Pacific Quay, with the in-house production team making CBBC's weekly jam-packed live magazine show *Saturday Mash-Up!* and *Bro's in Control*, where best mates Adam Beales and Joe Tasker battle to be the best, in the funniest grungiest games, as well as CBeebies' much loved pirate gameshow *Swashbuckle* and nature series *Chantelle and Rory's Teeny Tiny Creatures*.

BBC Alba caters for Scottish Gaelic speaking children, showing children's content for two hours every weekday, between 5pm and 7pm. The first hour is presented as 'CBeebies Alba' and the second hour as 'CBBC Alba'. *Meaban is Moo* is a gorgeous CBeebies Alba original series created by Warrick Brownlow-Pike, who you might be familiar with as the talented puppeteer behind Dodge T. Dog from the CBeebies House.

BBC ALBA also brings Gaelic broadcasting to the world through the European Broadcasting Union's (EBU) content-sharing scheme. BBC ALBA shares its children's drama and documentaries with other member broadcasters through an initiative that creates a prestigious, international showcase of some of the best children's content from across the world. BBC ALBA has been involved in the drama exchange for eight years and the documentary scheme for five years and have contributed eight dramas and five documentaries to the scheme, with Gaelic content being shown in more than 18 countries, including Finland, Spain, Japan and China.

Children's programmes in the Gaelic language have achieved recent awards success. In 2022 BBC ALBA's *Cùm Sùil Orm*, a story about a young refugee's reunion with his father, won the Royal

Courtesy of Terri Langam

Get Set Galactic

flying the flag for kid's TV. Plum Films makes the fantastic *Roots and Fruits* – the ultimate five (minutes) a day, starring fruit and veg performing and revealing fascinating facts about themselves in the most nutritious variety show around, and Marakids' recently adapted the adventures of Michael Bond's loveable guinea pig heroine *Olga da Polga* and her animal friends. Both series are currently on CBeebies.

Television Society (RTS) Scotland Award for Best Children's Programme. It was made by Corran Media based on the Isle of Lewis. This success followed on from 2019 RTS Scotland Best Children's Programme award winner, *Buidheagan*, which was commissioned as part of the EBU drama scheme and made by Sorbier Productions based in Glasgow.

Hello Halo Kids have also been recognised internationally. Last year our CBeebies series *Let's Go for A Walk* won the prestigious Prix Jeunesse award in the Up-to-6 nonfiction category and was first runner up for the Japan Prize International Contest for Educational Media in the Preschool Division.

We aren't short of brilliant animation studios up here: Interference Pattern, Wild Child Animation and Eyebolls to name but a few. All create awesome kid's content. There are also some fantastic Scottish production companies

The Sky Kids original series *The Brilliant World of Tom Gates*, created by and based on the books by Liz Pichon, is made by Wild Child Animation and Black Camel all based in Scotland. The series won the BAFTA Scotland Award for Entertainment. Unfortunately BAFTA Scotland doesn't have a category to celebrate Children's content in their annual awards, which is a frustrating and ongoing discussion I continue to have with them.

Children's TV being made in Scotland or featuring the children who live here is vital. Whether that's hearing an accent, the Gaelic language being spoken, recognising the places where they live, or taking part in a show, representation for Scottish children is so important, and I feel privileged to be making children's content up here.

"Mon the weans!"

Children's Television In Wales

Laura Sinclair, Doctoral Researcher, School of Journalism, Media and Culture, Cardiff University

Wales is a small but proud nation, with a fierce desire to protect our indigenous language, and children's television is central to this preservation. Welsh language public service broadcaster, S4C – Sianel Pedwar Cymru (meaning Channel 4 Wales), provides audiences in Wales with diverse and original content for children through the medium of the Welsh language. As with all PSBs, education is key to the provision. The two main services are *Cyw*, aimed at 3–6 year old children and *Stwnsh* aimed at the 7–13 year old age group. 39 hours per week of content is aired for the younger audience, with interactive apps and educational support available online for both children and parents. *Stwnsh* maintains regular weekday and Saturday morning scheduled slots. With a target of 1 million speakers by 2050 in the Welsh Government's sight, the broadcast media sector in Wales sees commissioning content in Welsh as a priority: to not only reach those existing Welsh speaking households, but those families sending their children to Welsh medium schools, who are not speakers themselves. Astoundingly at present, half of all viewing sessions on the Welsh BBC iPlayer are of children's programmes, with the majority of those targeted at preschool audiences (S4C, 2023), with S4C stating that in families with English speaking parents it is 'only through *Cyw* that they hear the Welsh language at home' (S4C, 2023). As with children's television across the UK, this PSB service provides a trusted educational and entertaining resource, which is important to both adults and children, particularly those from non-Welsh speaking backgrounds. Continuing educational services on their digital platforms, S4C also provides apps such as *Cywion Bach (Little Chicks)* which is an app designed to teach preschool children Welsh words alongside their parents through an interactive game, amongst many other services available to parents and children. *Cyw* also offers an educational magazine subscription, home learning resources and merchandise available through its website.

Alongside popular dubbed CBeebies content aired through the *Cyw* service such as *Bing, Patrôl Pawennau (Paw Patrol)* and *Blociau Rhif (Numberblocks)*, recognisable Welsh originals are available for children to watch, like *Sali Mali*. The animated series, which is an adaptation from Mary Vaughan Jones Welsh language books, launched in 2000 boasts a theme tune sung by Catatonia's Cerys Matthews and Hollywood star Rhys Ifans. *Sali Mali* has become an iconic media character and for many is a symbol of Welshness with merchandise for children often sold at key Welsh cultural sites, such as museums, and her stories being aired on television for generations of children to watch, as well as read. In Wales, children's media content plays a vital role in connecting audiences to the language and merchandise with Welsh media characters is a staple in educational institutions across Wales.

Stwnsh boasts a plethora of comedy, factual and documentary formats within its service for elder children, through both live action and animation. BAFTA Cymru Award Winner *Hei Hanes!* has been a particular success, presenting a mixture of old and new Wales, with characters exploring Welsh history through vlogging, recognising the need to represent Welsh culture and history, whilst also remaining relevant to its younger audience. This pre-teen age group is crucial to the success of audience retention and is a challenge for Welsh broadcasters to consider in their programme making when leaving the children's content and entering the adult landscape.

Since the golden age of children's television in the 1980's, Wales has had a reputation for producing some of the most recognisable children's television programmes on our television screens. Children's content has been a jewel in the crown of Welsh language broadcasting, with the first programme aired on S4C being *SuperTed* in 1982. *SuperTed* is noted as one of S4C's biggest success stories after being sold worldwide to over 120 countries and dubbed in over 30 languages. The superhero is also due to grace our screens again, with a remake of the classic show scheduled to be produced this year.

Fireman Sam (Sam Tân as he is known in Wales) and the stories told about the fictional village of Pontypandy (a mix of the towns of Pontypridd and Tonypandy) also had global success, reaching over 40 countries, and broadcast in not just Welsh and English, but Scottish Gaelic as well. Series 15 is due to be released this year,

with *Fireman Sam* still having a regular slot on Channel 5's Milkshake! Both shows enabled the growth of the creative industry sector within Wales providing independent companies with the opportunities to work on such programmes and inspiring others to locate here as Wales became recognised globally for its children's television output.

Wales still boasts notable television production companies, such as Boom Cymru (Boom Kids), Rondo Media, and Cwmni Da who are producing fantastic programmes for Wales' children on both S4C and English medium broadcasters. But as is the reoccurring issue across all children's television original production across the UK, there is the threat of lack of funding for original content. All three companies listed above received funding as part of the Young Audience's Content Fund (YACF) with S4C commissioning six programmes as a result of the fund, including our old faithful *Sali Mali*. With equality and diversity at its core, the YACF also highlighted the need for audience representation on screen by embedding an application framework that resulted in better diversity on screen, as well as employing a diverse range of people into the production teams behind the screen. With the YACF pilot not being continued, the Welsh Government's Young Content Fund announcement was welcome news to the sector, with funding available to successful Welsh independent companies to produce bilingual projects for young audiences.

The Well-being of Future Generations (Wales) Act 2015 encourages us all to think about Wales' ambition and wellbeing goals for the younger generations. One of its seven wellbeing goals is ensuring Wales maintains 'a vibrant culture and thriving Welsh language' (2015, p4) with the people of Wales being able to access their own culture as well as others. Central to this Act is creating a positive change for our future generations and this sentiment should be considered across children's television representation for the children of Wales. Although a thriving Welsh language output has been noted, representation of Welsh children on English language television is still lacking. It still seems somewhat rare to come across a Welsh accent on our children's screen, as in the refreshing exception of *My Petsaurus*. The need for representation of Wales and its people is important to showcase our small nation to the UK and globally and to also attract and maintain Welsh viewers. As across all UK nations, viewing of linear television in Wales has fallen since the pandemic by 12.6% but this is '…the largest proportion decrease of any UK nation' (Ofcom Media Nations Report, 2022). As is the trend across the UK, the Ofcom Media Nations report also discovered that younger audiences in Wales, aged between 4–15, watched the least amount of broadcast TV. It is important not only to understand that this is due to the threat and rise of digital platforms, such as YouTube and TikTok, but also to highlight the need to better understand why this is the case. Through research, it is often noted that children are moving away from linear television as they don't see people who sound or look like them on screen and children now have the power to create their own content to fill this gap in the market. Welsh children should be able to identify with the content on our television screens, to see and learn about Wales, which may also in turn inspire them to be a part of Wales' growing creative sector.

References

Ofcom (2022). *Media Nations: Wales 2022.* Available at: https://www.ofcom.org.uk/__data/assets/pdf_file/0019/242704/wales-report-2022.pdf

S4C (2023). *Children's Content.* Available at: https://www.s4c.cymru/en/production/page/26383/childrens-content/#

Well-being of Future Generations (Wales) Act 2015. Available at: https://www.futuregenerations.wales/wp-content/uploads/2017/01/WFGAct-English.pdf

Northern Ireland: A Unique Place For World Class Content

Gráinne McGuinness, Creative Director, Paper Owl Films Ltd

It's been a year of Dungeons, Dragons, Derry Girls, Oscars and BAFTAs in Northern Ireland. This is a place unique for its history, its beauty, its people and its stories. Perched on the edge of Europe, buffeted by the Atlantic Ocean and Irish Sea, it's easy to feel where our stories come from when you take in the view or speak to the people.

Stories

The stories of Northern Ireland weren't inspired by an always easy road – often forged in the fires of adversity, shaped and honed in the telling for new generations. Today our stories and talents take their place with audiences all around the world, for all ages and in all genres.

People

As childrens' content producers, we serve 100% of the future. Those of us privileged to do that strive for what is best for them – to make them laugh and sing and learn and grow through the content we produce. To help them see a better future for themselves and others. Take a look at any gathering of Northern Irish content creators and that's what you will see them doing amongst themselves: laughing, singing (often badly), learning from each other and growing an international industry that punches well above its weight in terms of the volume of amazing content that it produces.

It's not just our love of story or a shared passion for a better future that sees us bringing in awards and reaching audiences all over the world. We are supported.

Skills

The mix of home grown productions and large scale international collaborations in the region provides opportunities for an ever growing talent pool. There are strong links with Ulster University and Northern Ireland Screen, offering industry placements and professional

Image by Rochak Shukla on Freepik

development schemes. 2023 saw the launch of NI Screen's new four-year strategy 'Stories, Skills and Sustainability', which sees the agency doubling down on its support for the local industry. Strong plans to futureproof the screen industry see investment in the next generation of professionals through industry led learning and work experience opportunities and supporting the continued professional development of experienced professionals. Skills development and great talent are key to the growth of the creative industries here and with a skills budget from Northern Ireland Screen of £4m per annum, there is planned, sustained support for growth.

Partnerships

Attractive development and production funding offers local companies the opportunity to grow their own IP and also to attract partnerships and collaborations from around the world to work in Northern Ireland. We are delighted to see so many productions find ways to get their own precious ideas made through collaborations that are supported practically and have a strong infrastructure to rely on.

Collaboration throughout the island of Ireland brings great advantages in terms of talent and financing opportunities – it's perfect for co-production and availing of tax credits and public funds and maximises the opportunities with talent, ideas and stories.

Northern Ireland is a unique place and unique in the screen industries, not least because of the funding opportunities that it has access to. Northern Ireland Screen, UK Tax Credit, BFI and BAI help us get our own IP into production and provide real opportunities for strategic partnerships in the region. We are open for business.

Talk to any of our companies: Dog Ears, Jam Media, Sixteen South, Paper Owl, ALT Animation, Taunt and others about collaboration opportunities. These are all amazing creative companies producing stand-out content for broadcasters in the UK and Ireland and punching way above their weight in a competitive international marketplace.

Sustainability

We are surrounded by the sea here, never far away from a green field and we are charged with protecting the audience we serve – that 100% of the future one. The BBC's Albert calculator is such a help to companies with this – creating a set of instructions and measurements to get started and show you how to make an impact with really simple steps. Sustainability is about an industry that is funded and planned to grow but with such a stunning backdrop, the need to make our content in sustainable ways is a very high priority.

Inclusivity

Inclusivity is very close to the hearts of our childrens' content producers. There's no getting away from the fact that this is a region of widespread socio economic disadvantage and we have a 'history'. But I think that's also why we work so hard for a better future for our young audiences. We do that through content that ensures all kinds of children are seen on screen and feel inspired to engage with the world in all kinds of ways. In our crews and in our content we are working ever harder to ensure that for our audiences that there is representation, access to opportunity for all and the inspiration to make all kinds of friends. This comes through the content we create and in the way that we create it.

Fighting To Keep Up With Children And Young Audiences: Reflections On Danish Children's Television In The 2020s

Dr Eva Novrup Redvall, Associate Professor and Head of the Section for Film Studies and Creative Media Industries, University of Copenhagen and **Dr Pia Majbritt Jensen**, Associate Professor, Department of Media Studies and Journalism, and Director, Centre for Transnational Media Research, Aarhus University

"The moment we think that we know all the answers, it is time to start asking the children again."

This is just one of the many statements from industry practitioners in our current research project on fiction for children and young audiences that illustrates the sense that it can be hard and stressful work keeping up with the interests and media use of children and young audiences today. Our 'Reaching Young Audiences' project (based at the University of Copenhagen) analyses the current strategies for commissioning, writing and producing fictional content for children, tweens and teens as well as their actual media use. The focus is on the Danish film and television industries, but we make comparisons with other countries with traditions for public service television for children, such as the UK, Australia and the neighbouring Scandinavian countries.

While, for many years, it was rather easy to reach the eyeballs of Danish children and adolescents in a mediascape dominated by national public service broadcasting and with many relatively popular domestic films, this exclusive access to the national audiences has become increasingly challenged in the 2020s with the arrival of many more screens, platforms and content providers in Denmark. Young audiences, for example, have access to an average of between four and five streaming services each and spend an average of approximately 90 minutes on social media each day, compared to only 20 minutes on traditional television.

A large part of our research is based on interviewing industry practitioners and observing industry events in order to study what is presented and perceived as best practice in producing successful public service content in an on-demand age – with an abundance of content on many different platforms constantly available. This has led to many interesting studies and findings, including: what are regarded as 'the ingredients of a streaming hit for kids' and working with 'junior editors' on new strategies for co-creating content with tweens and teens (Redvall and Christensen, 2021), as well as arguing that detailed ethnographic research with children is needed if one is to make appealing content for them in the current media landscape (Freudendal, 2022).

Across the board one has the sense that making content for children and young audiences is currently based on listening to them and (more or less desperately) trying to keep up with what is going on in their lives. To some extent, writers, producers and commissioners always draw on widespread industry lore, as well as their own childhood memories and knowledge of specific children around them, and there are definitely still many public service and media literacy ambitions behind the making of new children's content. But there is also a general acknowledgement that one should carefully listen to and involve young audiences to get their attention, and this goes for the making of content as well as its distribution. As an example, should one push content through traditional marketing channels or rather let audiences find and pull content themselves, as was the case with the successful Norwegian serial *SKAM* that wanted young audiences to discover and share the show without adult interference? As another example, a mantra in the Danish industry is to try to be on the platforms where young audiences are, but how should public service broadcasters navigate, for instance, TikTok?

As in many other countries, there are numerous challenges to address as a small nation, with a public service broadcaster wanting to reach young audiences, both with regard to production and distribution of content. The 2020s have seen many major changes in the overall framework for making children's content at the Danish Broadcasting Corporation (DR), such as a new and very popular content 'universe' for the 1–3 year olds (DR Minisjang, launched in 2021), which also led to a change in the age groups of the two existing children's channels – to targeting 4–8 year olds (DR Ramasjang, previously 3–6 year olds) and 9–14 year olds (DR Ultra, previously 7–12 year olds). While DR had previously not produced content for 'viewers in diapers' based on the conviction that they should not be watching screens, this meant DR had to commit to developing a whole new content universe – which quickly became popular, with 30% of the 1–3 year olds watching on a weekly basis already in 2021 and several productions reaching the top of the charts on DR's streaming site. These changes in target audiences have also led to DR reaching out, through DR Ultra, to the younger teenagers who had previously had little content produced specifically for them.

Another example of a major recent change within children's television is DR's introduction of *FredagsTamTam* (*Friday Bang Bang*), a 60 minute long cartoon compilation show with a majority of Danish and other Nordic cartoons, that in 2023 replaced the long-running *Disney Sjov* (*Disney Fun*), which – as the name reveals – was the Danish version of the US *Disney Afternoon* and had been a Friday night tradition among Danish families with children for 31 years. This change of programming means that substantial funding is being spent on boosting the Danish and wider Nordic animation industry, whilst more independence from global children's media players like the Disney Corporation is being encouraged.

Major changes in the overall broadcasting framework, programming strategies and training schemes, such as the ones mentioned above, naturally have consequences for what is on offer and produced for children and young audiences. Many of these changes build on extensive research involving various experts, such as developmental and child psychologists in the case of Minisjang. Drawing on expert knowledge and conducting research when it comes to children's content is far from a new phenomenon, but it has been remarkable to see the way in which analyses and reports on children and young audiences have become a major point of reference in the Danish film and television industries during the early 2020s. With a key challenge being to try and keep up with the interests, concerns and media preferences of children and young audiences – and figure out the best ways to translate and use these findings when creating and circulating new fictional content for them. Most recently, AI and chatbots are rapidly becoming a part of children's media lives, leaving schools and higher education, as well as content producers, actively considering the implications on a wider scale.

Testament to the fact that the young audiences arguably constitute a burning issue for the domestic media institutions is the fact that, in Denmark, the average age of a child getting their first smartphone is just 9 years old. This means that, from then on, children quickly become independent media consumers and, often, also highly skilled media content producers. A recent report for the Danish Film Institute (DFI) found that Danish children love *producing* films as part of their school curriculum – and are very good at it, most often better and more knowledgeable than their teachers – but are less fond of *watching* films at school (DFI, 2023). Gaming is another area where children, especially boys, play together with their friends – and outside the realm of their parents. In fact, gaming has become an important facilitator of boys' social lives and communities and, as such, a direct competitor to watching films and series. When 9–14 year old Danish children were asked (again by the DFI) what they would prefer to do if they had three hours of free time to spare, the majority of boys would rather play video games than go to the cinema.

In our own research we also identified another key issue. Based on a national survey among Danish 8–17 year olds and qualitative ethnographies with 20 children in the same age group, we found a clear preference for global US streaming services, as well as US films and series. This preference is in fact so strong that US streaming services (such as Netflix and Disney+) and US content can be regarded as the standard and benchmark, as opposed to the nonstandard (or maybe even, according to our respondents, *sub*-standard) domestic services and content (Jensen, et al., 2021).

As the quote at the opening of this article illustrates, many industry practitioners find that producing content for children is currently a constant process of finding out what is on children's minds and how they interact with many different media forms in a complex interplay between national and international programmes, platforms and players. Producing good children's content has always meant taking a genuine interest in children and their lives, but the pace of change does seem to be striking and a topic that is very alive. Even when industry practitioners try to adapt, unforeseen developments can quickly challenge any new strategy, as illustrated when the Norwegian public service broadcaster NRK made the serial *Toxic* for TikTok in the autumn of 2022 – only to see the use of TikTok banned by the NRK and several other broadcasters and institutions in the spring of 2023. As argued by media scholar David Hesmondhalgh, the cultural and media industries are always marked by an intricate balance between change and continuity. When it comes to keeping up with children and young audiences, the 2020s have definitely seen many changes in the approach to making public service television – and no one claims to have all the right answers.

More information about **The Reaching Young Audiences** *research project (financed by Independent Research Fund Denmark, grant: 9037-00145B) can be found here:*

https://comm.ku.dk/research/film-science-and-creative-media-industries/rya/

References

Danish Film Institute. (2023). *Close-up A study of 7–18-year-olds and their lives with films, series, and social media*

Freudendal, J. (2022). Working with 'Kidnographers' to not be cringe: New ways of using ethnographic audience research methods when trying to reach young audiences. In: *CSTonline*

Jensen, P. M., Mitric, P., Larsen, T. S. and Mouritsen, A. S. (2021). *What is Quality Audiovisual Fiction as Seen through the Eyes of Young Danish Viewers: Results from an Explorative Survey of 8-17-Year-Old Children.* Report from Aarhus University and University of Copenhagen

Jensen, P. M. andMitric, P. (Forthcoming 2023). The appeal of public service fiction in an internationalised media context. In: (Eds) P. M. Jensen, E. N. Redvall and C. L. Christensen, *Audiovisual content for children and adolescents in The Nordics.* Nordicom

Redvall, E. N. and Christensen, K. B. (2021). Co-creating content with children to avoid 'Uncle Swag': Strategies for producing public service television drama for tweens and teens at the Danish children's channel DR Ultra. In: *Critical Studies in Television*, 16(2)

It's A Picnic Basket, Not A Fridge?
Strategies From Norway For Reaching A New Media Generation

Dr Vilde Schanke Sundet, Associate Professor in Media and Communication, Oslo Metropolitan University

TikTok, YouTube, Instagram, and Snapchat dominate the media life of many teenagers. These platforms are natural go-to services for young people seeking entertainment, and they filter content from friends, peers, legacy media rooted in mass media *and* a growing industry of social media entertainers – content creators, influencers, online celebrities, and digital profiles. Unlike older generations – whose formative years were situated in homogenous and national media landscapes (Bolin, 2017) – younger people today grow up in a media landscape where global entertainment platforms are an essential part of their everyday life.

Today's youth are not the first generation to come of age in an increasingly globalised media landscape or with new media technologies. Yet their media habits *may* mark a generational shift in which today's teens will not adopt or adapt over time to the media habits of older generations. Like no generation before them, today's teens can, if they want, avoid domestic media simply because the entertainment content offered elsewhere is so massive and immersive. Industry descriptions such as the 'lost generation' and the 'youth challenge' signal how legacy media perceive re-engagement with young audiences as core to their future legitimacy and existence (Sundet & Lüders, 2022). *If* a generational shift occurs, it will have significant consequences, not only for national legacy media and policymakers regulating the media industry but also for young people, their identity, work and feelings of belonging.

These issues are at the heart of our research project, *Global Natives? Serving Young Audiences on Global Media Platforms*. The project is funded by the Norwegian Research Council and includes researchers from the University of Oslo, the University of Bergen, King's College London and the Norwegian Institute of Social Research. We focus on media entertainment defined broadly, including content produced by legacy media players and by content creators, influencers, online celebrities and profiles. Empirical studies include national audience surveys, qualitative interviews with Norwegian teenagers, industry workers and policymakers, case studies and document analysis of key institutional and policy texts. The project aims to study whether the media habits of Norwegian teens today mark a generational shift and, if so, what that means for young people themselves, the entertainment industry and the regulation of youth media.

We use the term 'global native' conceptually – and provocatively – to address sociologically and empirically how teenagers today grow up as a generation. Being born into a global media culture does not mean however teenagers have congenital 'global' characteristics. The question is how the 'global' – a central part of young people's everyday media life – is included in what shapes their world orientation and what it means for them to grow up and have their formative years taking place at a time when global platforms, social media and on-demand content are already assumed, rather adapted to.

We are also interested in what the changing media life of teenagers means for content producers seeking to attract them. In a previous interview study with CEOs and top-level executives from the Norwegian film, television, music and book industries, we found that industry workers are very keen to attract young people and understand their habits and interests (Sundet & Lüders, 2022). More specifically, we found industry workers to share a collective understanding of young people as having unique media habits and being avid users of streaming and 'new' digital media services. Youth were often perceived as challenging to reach but essential to understand since their preferences were foretelling for the media habits and industry logic of the near future. We found some notable differences between industries, but there was a clear overarching perception of young audiences: they were seen to represent a new media generation. To attract their attention, industry players needed to play by their rules.

In a current follow-up study, we again interview industry workers to investigate how they respond to the 'youth challenge'. Here we also included representatives from the emerging social media entertainment industry – content creators, influencers and online profiles – and profile agencies and intermediaries. The study points to at least three commonly used strategies used by Norwegian industry workers to attract and re-connect with young audiences.

The first strategy we call '*youth know youth best*'. It builds on the premise that young people make up a distinct new generation, hard to understand and often hard to serve, especially by older generations out of touch with teens' everyday life. One industry executive explained: "Good entertainment for me and my son is two completely different things". Hence, a natural go-to approach was to employ young people to make and spread youth content. One informant relievedly explained: "We are fortunate because we have young staff. We have the luxury of creating things *we* think are fun". Another approach was to build on audience research to get insight into young people's everyday life and use local familiarity and relevance as a critical advantage in the competition with global players. This approach represents a general 'audience turn' in much Nordic youth television, often exemplified by the teen drama *SKAM*, well known for its massive use of audience insight to serve the specific demographic segment of Norwegian 16 year old girls. In *SKAM*, the audience research included more than 50 in-depth interviews with Norwegian teens from across the country, 200 speed interviews, school visions, social media scanning and the readings of reports and statistics on teen culture.

The second strategy we call '*lending fame and adopting talent*'. This strategy uses already popular content creators, influencers and online profiles to learn from their social media experiences and use their fame to appeal to the youth market. As such, the strategy reflects a well-known advertising method where brands use celebrities as ambassadors to benefit from their fame and status. Several executives addressed the increasing use of influencers and online celebrities in legacy media productions seeking to reach the young. Many also addressed the new skills and talents needed to succeed in a changing media landscape. One informant explained: "Today's new talents are not presenters reading cue cards on television. They are content *creators* and have grown up experimenting on social media". While lending fame and adopting talent for some was seen as a natural next step allowing new types of entertainment universes, others saw it as more troublesome and paved with complex dilemmas. For the latter group, this strategy was often described as driven by necessity, implying that doing 'nothing' would come with high costs. Many also echoed the influencer trope that 'people follow people', meaning that investing in big profiles would be an efficient way to get attention and make 'people turn on the telly'.

The third strategy, we call '*bring back*'. The aim here is to use social media expansions and online profiles to create a relationship with young people where they are currently engaging with content and (hopefully!) channel them back to legacy media platforms. This strategy includes making and sharing content on social media to create buzz, attention and, most importantly, a relationship with hard-to-get teenagers. This strategy was also often legitimised by necessity and informed by slogans such as 'you have to be where the audience is'. As one industry executive explained: "We need to be attractive for every

new generation. If not, we risk being irrelevant in the future". Another used the metaphor of the picnic basket to illustrate her point about the changing media world: "We used to fill the fridge, and then young people came to us. Today, we must fill the picnic basket and go where they are. They don't visit us by themselves. If they are on TikTok, we must talk to them on TikTok".

All three strategies have challenges and dilemmas, which the executives were hasty to address. For most legacy media, massive use of third-party platforms is problematic as it contests editorial decisions and challenges trust and control. Prominent use of influencers and online profiles likewise represents dilemmas regarding commercial bindings and exploitative collaborations. Furthermore, these strategies might also build on biased perceptions of youth as audiences and a new generation. Hence, they should be critically examined and studied. For instance, while it may be true that young people know young people, it is also true that experienced content creators and storytellers know good content, even for young audiences.

References

Bolin, G. (2017). *Media generations: Experience, identity and mediatised social change.* Routledge

Sundet, V. S. and Lüders, M. (2022). 'Young people are on YouTube': Industry notions on streaming and youth as a new media generation. In: *Journal of Media Business Studies*

WHAT CMF DOES IS IMPORTANT WORK

The way our children see themselves reflected across their media experiences is fundamental in defining their view of the world, their values and their aspirations.

This is why the Children's Media Foundation has never been more important and we are incredibly proud to support the brilliant work you do.

Keep doing it.

INSIGHT | STRATEGY | CREATIVE

KIDSINDUSTRIES.COM

We're a full-service marketing agency that specialises in the family market.

Bernard Cribbins OBE

1928–2023

Bernard Cribbins, who sadly died in 2022 aged 93, had a remarkable career on stage, in film, and on TV where, as well as appearing in many series ranging from *Dr Who* to *Fawlty Towers*, he became known as a great children's performer and storyteller.

Many adults will remember him as the kindly railway porter Mr Perks in the 1970 *The Railway Children* who befriends the three Waterbury children, led by Roberta (Bobbie) played by Jenny Agutter, who find themselves in Yorkshire with a mystery to solve.

However, it was as a solo TV storyteller that Bernard became known to many generations of children. He was a regular on the long running daily 15 minute BBC storytelling programme *Jackanory* (1965–96) and held the record for telling the most stories – 114 titles – despite strong competition from Kenneth Williams!

Bernard told/read a wide range of stories including classics like *Alice in Wonderland* and *Alice Through The Looking Glass*, modern classics like Roald Dahl's *Charlie and the Chocolate Factory*, and *James and the Giant Peach*, plus stories specially written for *Jackanory*. He told all the very funny *Arabel and Mortimer* stories (Mortimer was Arabel's pet raven) written by Joan Aiken and beautifully illustrated by Quentin Blake. Bernard was

also the narrator of the animated series *The Wombles*, and later in his career returned to CBeebies as the storyteller Jack in the series *Old Jack's Boat* (2013–15).

Telling or reading stories to children on television isn't easy. It should feel like an individual experience for the viewer – the story is being told directly to *you*. Bernard excelled at this. His storytelling was a one-to-one relationship. We saw this first hand when Bernard kindly recorded a personal tribute for the Children's Media Foundations 50th Anniversary celebration for *Jackanory* in 2015.

"Ah yes, there you are!"

In his early film career Bernard had a leading role as a companion to Peter Cushing's Dr Who in the 1966 film *Daleks – Invasion Earth 2050*. It was this that led to Russell T. Davies casting Bernard as Wilf Mott, Catherine Tate's grandfather, in his revival of the *Dr Who* franchise, which brought a whole new body of fans and appreciation. Not least from Children's Media Foundation patron Russell himself, who said of Bernard, "I'm so lucky to have known him… A legend has left the world".

Bernard was a lovely man with a great sense of humour and warmth. Those of us who worked with him were privileged. We will remember him.

Remembered by **Anna Home OBE**, Chair, The Children's Media Foundation

Lloyd Morrisett and Newton N. Minow

1929–2023

1926–2023

Two media icons passed away in the first months of 2023: Newton N. Minow and Lloyd Morrisett. In their time, each spoke a single sentence that changed the direction of American children's television and public service media.

In May 1961, Minow was the newly-appointed chair of the Federal Communications Commission. In his first speech to the National Association of Broadcasters (NAB), he challenged its members to watch an entire day of network television, closing with "I can assure you that what you will observe is a vast wasteland."

In February 1966, at a New York dinner party, Morrisett – then Vice President of the Carnegie Corporation of New York – asked host Joan Ganz Cooney, "do you think television can be used to teach young children?" She replied that she wasn't sure, but would like to find out. Three months later, Cooney delivered to Morrisett a report titled *The Potential Uses of Television in Pre-School Education*.

That report – much of which still holds up today – led to funding for the development and launch of Sesame Street, still in production 53 years later and with co-productions worldwide.

Minow: the unintended wasteland

Minow thought "vast wasteland" would be a sidenote in his address. The words he meant to be remembered were "public interest". Recall that the evolution of media in the US ran opposite of the UK, where public broadcasting was well established before commercial services were introduced. In America, commercial radio and television came first.

Whether it was the sting of "vast wasteland" or the exhortation to "public interest", Minow's speech did spark action. By 1965, the Carnegie Commission on Educational Television was launched, congress passed the Public Broadcasting Act in 1967, *Mister Rogers' Neighborhood* debuted locally in Pittsburgh in 1966 and nationally on the National Educational Television network, and the offspring of the Morrisett-Cooney dinner conversation was in production – *Sesame Street*.

Morrisett: transforming jingles

Lloyd Morrisett studied experimental psychology; his focus at the Carnegie Corporation was on early education. The question he asked Joan Ganz Cooney, though, was driven by observation at home, where he noted that his toddler daughter was able to memorize every advertising jingle she heard on TV. Perhaps that same stickiness could be applied to learning school-readiness concepts like literacy and numeracy. Further, Morrisett believed that a national television program might have the scale to close the achievement gap between lower- and middle-class children, reaching children in communities with few early learning opportunities.

The project could not have been better timed: in the mid-1960s, President Lyndon Johnson's 'Great Society' initiatives were addressing three key elements underpinning *Sesame Street* – eliminating poverty, reforming civil rights and expanding educational opportunities.

Morrisett was not only in a position to support development of *Sesame Street* at the Carnegie Corporation, he had the connections to pull in other funders. Still, he was hardly a hands-off benefactor. Morrisett became board chair of the nascent Children's Television Workshop.

Lasting public service legacies

Neither Minow nor Morrisett stepped back from advocacy for public service media after their initial moments of éclat.

Morrisett coined the term 'digital divide'. Noting a divergence in society along cultural and racial lines spans online and offline: between the information 'haves' and 'have-nots'.

Minow served on the boards of National Educational Television and PBS (including as its chair) helping to secure federal funds for *Sesame Street* from that seat. He was for a time President of the Carnegie Corporation, *Sesame*'s original funder.

Set aside "vast wasteland" and focus on "public service". Newton Minow wanted to build, not tear down, TV – especially for children. Minow's daughter Nell noted that "even though he's famous for complaining about what was wrong with TV, he really delighted in what was right about TV."

The American Children's Television Festival

I was fortunate to interact with both Morrisett and Minow. They were incredibly busy people, but never hesitated to support the American Children's Television Festival, which I ran in the early 1990s. Both served as board members for the competition (modeled after the international PRIX JEUNESSE). Lloyd Morrisett made the first development grant via Markle; Newton Minow, as executor of puppeteer Burr Tillstrom's estate, secured the rights to call our contest the Ollie Awards, after the irrepressible dragon of *Kukla, Fran and Ollie*.

There are many routes to supporting the public interest in media, especially for children. Some dream and create, some educate and mentor, some advocate or lobby, some put up the funding. Seldom will you ever find two visionaries who opt for all of the above, using every available avenue to lead us from the "vast wasteland" to "where the air is sweet."

Remembered by **David Kleeman**, SVP, Dubit

David Sutherland

1933–2023

David, Dave, Sutherland, the artist who gave life to some of Britain's best-loved comic characters died in January 2023, aged 89. He was the creative force behind *The Beano's Bash Street Kids* from 1962 until his last comic strip which appeared in the Beano shortly after his death.

I had the great pleasure of meeting Dave at the offices of *The Beano's* publisher, DC Thomson, in Dundee a number of times. He wasn't working in the office, or just popping in for a chat, rather he was hand delivering the 'pencils' of his weekly *The Bash Street Kids* strips, something he did every week without fail. He was a tall, shy man with a huge smile and a beautiful, softly spoken Invergordon accent. I clearly remember feeling in awe meeting a living legend and watching *The Beano* comic team treat him with such warm reverence, as he gladly showed me his latest strip, explaining the plot out loud.

David started working for DC Thomson in 1959 and had been drawing *The Bash Street Kids* since 1962, making him the single most important illustrator in *Beano* history. David also drew *Dennis the Menace* for over two decades, and *Biffo the Bear*, which he took over from his hero, Dudley D. Watkins.

David was born in Invergordon, Scotland, in 1933, the youngest of three children. As soon as he left school, David joined Rex Studios in Glasgow where he learned the art trade, illustrating adverts for all manner of products. While there he attended evening classes at Glasgow School of Art to add to his qualifications.

He illustrated cinema advertising posters and was the only artist approved to draw Disney characters in the UK. He also created street posters of the royal family, which were displayed around Glasgow for the late Queen's Coronation in 1953.

In 1959, David entered a drawing competition organised by DC Thomson. His artwork made such an impression that he was invited to illustrate adventure strips for *The Beano*. David began work on *Beano* adventure strips such as *Danny on a Dolphin* and *The Great Flood of London*.

His ability and versatility were obvious to the editor and soon he was working on some of *Beano's* most famous strips as an understudy to the established comic greats. By 1970, David was the mainstay of the comic, drawing *Biffo the Bear* on the cover, *The Bash Street Kids* in the centre spread and *Dennis & Gnasher* on the back cover. He drew well over a thousand episodes of Britain's favourite wild child, Dennis, over a 28 year period from 1970 until 1998.

But it was on *The Bash Street Kids* that he would create his greatest legacy. David replaced Leo Baxendale on the strip in 1962 and produced his final illustration at the end of 2022, for publication the following week.

Over the years he drew well over 3,500 individual instalments in the comic as well as another 500 annuals and other specials. Generations of children across the UK have lapped up David's uniquely observed, beautifully drawn and supremely funny comic strips. Our thanks and condolences go to David's family and friends.

[Insert photo credit]

Remembered by **Emma Scott**, Former CEO, Beano Studios

Raymond Briggs

1934–2022

It was a huge honour and a privilege to work with Raymond Briggs, first on *The Snowman and The Snowdog*, a sequel to the much-loved TV special *The Snowman*, and later on an animated feature film adaptation of his graphic novel about his parents, *Ethel & Ernest*.

Raymond was an incredible author and illustrator and his books lend themselves perfectly to animated adaptations. His eye for detail was phenomenal and he conveyed such truth and honesty in his very economical yet intricate drawings that they represent a universality of human emotion. Raymond never talked down to children or under-estimated them and as a result his books continue to entertain and delight children and adults alike.

We were first introduced to Raymond by his long-time collaborator John Coates, producer of the original film adaptation of *The Snowman*, as well as *When The Wind Blows*, *Father Christmas* and *The Bear*. John was famous for his long boozy lunches and it was at one of these that we first got to know Raymond.

Working with Raymond on *Ethel & Ernest*, a film about a very ordinary English couple living through the tumultuous events of the 20th century, was a very emotional experience. Raymond spent the entire voice-recording session with Jim Broadbent and Brenda Blethyn, who played his mum and dad, in floods of tears. He said

afterwards that he felt as if his parents were back in the room with him. He often welled up watching the film and said that although he loved it, he had to ration the number of times he watched it as it made him so emotional. When we released *Ethel & Ernest* both Lupus Films and Raymond received sackfuls of letters, as well as emails, tweets and Facebook posts from people saying "they remind me so much of my parents/grandparents" or "that was just like my childhood". The film won awards at festivals around the world, and at one festival in Morocco it was given the audience award by a group of teenagers due to its emotional punch and the fact that Ethel and Ernest reminded them of their own grandparents.

Raymond had a famously curmudgeonly public profile but in fact he was a sensitive and kind person who cared little for the trappings of fame but was incredibly generous with his time and always appreciative of the artists who worked to adapt his books into animated films. He would tell the animators that he was in awe of their talents and could never do their job himself. He always welcomed us to his home in West Sussex with tea and biscuits and loved a laugh and a practical joke. We made a point of meeting him for lunch on his birthday each year, until sadly the pandemic got in the way.

Raymond was a unique talent and a truly lovely man and all of us at Lupus Films miss him very much.

Remembered by **Camilla Deakin**, Producer, Lupus Films

PLANT

CONTENT FOR CHILDREN
WITH CHILDREN
BY CHILDREN

CYNNWYS

Ceidiog

CONTENT

The Arthur Humberstone Animation Archive

Nigel Humberstone, film music composer

Nigel and his twin brother Klive are currently cataloguing and looking at ways to preserve and present the content of their late father's archive.

When our late father, Arthur Humberstone, died on the eve of the millennium, little did we know or anticipate that we were to inherit a historical animation archive.

Arthur Humberstone (1912–1999) was a British animator, artist and director whose credits include *Animal Farm, Yellow Submarine* and *The BFG*. He worked with Halas & Batchelor and as a senior animator with Martin Rosen on *Watership Down* and *The Plague Dogs*.

Arthur Humberstone's influence is evident throughout the collection, which we now privately manage, as it contains a wealth of pre-production materials spanning his 45 year career. The archive reveals the profound influence he had over animal aesthetics whilst enhancing our understanding and appreciation of animation history.

Courtesy of the Arthur Humberstone Animation Archive

Arthur Humberstone

Growing up in the 70s, it was ordinary everyday life for us to pass the door of our father's pencil-scented home studio and observe him sitting at his angled light box desk – drawing, sketching and flipping his hand-drawn animations. We didn't know any different and never truly comprehended the significance of the reams of drawings, storyboards, painted cels, sketches, and associated memorabilia that lay stacked on the metal shelving in his room.

If, like myself, you believe that the essence of any work produced is contained within its production methods, then archives like these are invaluable and need to be preserved to document and tell the wider picture of animation history.

From starting relatively late in life as a trainee at G.B Animation's Moor Hall facility, Arthur Humberstone went on to become a prolific animator. He had worked well beyond retirement into the late 1980s, by which point computer animation, the digital successor to frame-by-frame animation, had started to influence the way animated films were made. As a proponent of old-school animation methods, he must have felt a sense of redundancy as his career finished, and it is a wonder he kept hold of so much archive material.

For us, it was not immediately obvious what lay within the seemingly meaningless piles of paperwork, its relevance, or why it should be preserved. Who would have known that an animator (like our father), who was involved with such a landmark production as England's first animated feature *Animal Farm* (1954, dir. John Halas and Joy Batchelor), had saved such a wealth of animation ephemera. Transient items like work charts, scene synopsis, monthly progress reports (including output, bonus system and timekeeping), so-called daily 'sweatbox notes' along with a visually rich collection from *Watership Down* (1976-1978) including interoffice memorandums, the likes of which help detail the inner workings of an animated feature production. Why someone would actively choose to retain items like progress reports is a mystery but, for enthusiasts and researchers, we are richer as a result.

As I have mentioned, it is a wonder that this archive survives – for one particular project, the 10-minute *Noddy Goes To Toyland* (1963), the contract stated that on completion "all physical material

prepared and used in the making of the pilot film and the main titling including all backgrounds, cells, artwork, sound-track recordings, music recordings, and other such materials" be returned. Luckily our father retained various pieces – mainly as a keepsake of his passionate, hard work – otherwise, there would be very little to document this moment in animation.

The Arthur Humberstone Animation Archive also highlights some interesting insights into the evolution of the characters of the *Watership Down* rabbits. Early character sheets, attributed to layout artist Gordon Harrison, depict the sizing of the rabbits but offer little facial identity or uniqueness. Whereas the comparative sizes model sheet, bearing Arthur's distinctive signature, shows a re-working towards the individual characterisation we know and love from the film. Arthur's signature on subsequent character sheets suggests he was a key influencer in their visual development.

Courtesy of the Arthur Humberstone Animation Archive

Throughout production at Nepenthe Studio, internal office memos would be circulated amongst the animation team, feeding them with essential guidelines, pointers and instructions. Retained by Humberstone, they offer a seldom-seen insight into the workings of a feature animated production. Even these memos were not exempt from the ever-present studio banter as one example, with what we can only assume is a forged Martin Rosen signature, pokes fun at Humberstone's habit of singing at his desk.

Other hidden gems include rare painted cels from the early production, *Nasrudin*, Richard William's ill-fated animated fantasy which later became *The Thief and the Cobbler* (1993). These materials demand further verification and research as do the remnants from almost 200 TV and cinema adverts, educational and short films that our father was involved with during his career.

Only in retrospect, and with the value of hindsight, do we appreciate what has been saved and we are keen to preserve, protect and share it as best we can. The post-war rebirth of British animation via Gaumont-British Animation, established at Moor Hall, Berkshire, in 1946, remains largely undocumented. However, archive materials allow a bringing to life of the facility as a fascinating forerunner that helped feed the burgeoning British animation industry with a wealth of writers, background artists, animators, painters, editors and camera technicians. Plans are underway to secure funding that will allow the archive to be properly digitised and make the collection available for researchers and enthusiasts alike.

Contributors

Vanessa Amberleigh

Vanessa Amberleigh has worked in Children's TV for nearly 35 years beginning her career in the theatre and going on to be a presenter on *Playdays*. Vanessa developed a passion for writing and creating kids content so moved behind the camera. She has worked for most of the major broadcasters and big independent companies as a writer, script editor, producer and exec. She is currently working part-time for Sky Kids and across independent projects.

Dr Cyrine Amor

Cyrine is a Senior Analyst in the commissioning team at Ampere Analysis, a London-based data and analytics firms specialising in the media and entertainment sector. She has authored several reports on genre- and market-specific commissioning activity as well as on IP-based content. Before joining Ampere in 2021, she worked as analyst for Screen Digest/IHS, as well as in film development at the UK Film Council. Cyrine holds a PhD in media and communications from Goldsmiths, University of London.

Steven Andrew

Steven started at the BBC, then became Controller of Granada Media Kid in 1999 followed by Commissioning Editor CITV 2004 and then Controller of Daytime ITV. He returned to CBBC in 2009 as Head of CBBC In-House Productions, overseeing a raft of content across all genres and platforms including award winning *Tracy Beaker Returns*, *Newsround Special*, *Blue Peter*, *Sadie J*, *Project Parent*, *Serious Livingstone* and *Just William*. He became Creative Director, Zodiak Kids TV in 2013, Exec Producing the BAFTA award winning interactive comedy *Secret Life of Boys*, CITV's *Spy School*, *Scrambled*, and award winning CBBC drama, *Joe All Alone*, *Flatmates* and the award winning sci-fi mystery adventure *Silverpoint*.

Laverne Antrobus

Laverne Antrobus is a Consultant Child and Educational Psychologist working at The Tavistock Clinic and Portman NHS Foundation Trust and for over 25 years has worked with children and families in the most need of help.

Laverne is regularly asked to give a psychological perspective on issues that affect children and their families on TV, radio and print. She has made programmes on childhood for the BBC, Channel 4 and Channel 5 and has recently created content to address children's mental health and key issues, like Coronovirus, BLM and climate change that impact on children's lives for the BBC's *Newsround* and Sky's *FYI*.

Rachel Bardill

Rachel Bardill has had a 20 year career as a senior leader in the children's digital media space in the UK. She creates impact with a clear vision and exceptional leadership skills to drive teams to success. She has a deep understanding of product and brand strategy across all digital touchpoints. Rachel leads large teams in an ever-moving digital landscape to drive the best results for brands and the business. Most recently she has spearheaded the BBC's first endeavour into *Roblox* for one of our most loved children's brands to test how we can build awareness and attribution of BBC iPlayer for our 7–12 audience. She has also led digital commissioning and brand strategy for some of the UK's biggest shows like *Blue Peter*, *Hey Duggee*, *Horrible Histories*, *Numberblocks* and much more. Her latest role as Senior Vice President, Marketing at The Insights Family has just begun and she can't wait to work alongside this amazing company.

Mike Batt

Mike Batt is a singer, songwriter, composer and producer, best known for creating The Wombles pop group and writing songs for the likes of Art Garfunkel, Cliff Richard and David Essex. Mike also composed, arranged and conducted the music for the 1999 *Watership Down* TV series. In 2020, his novel *THE CHRONICLES OF DON'T BE SO RIDICULOUS VALLEY* was published. Mike has recently arranged and conducted string arrangements for new releases from pop acts Olly Murs, Mimi Webb and Scarlet Opera, and is currently engaged in a creative and business partnership with French singer-songwriter-entrepreneur Jean-Charles Capelli.

Dr Cary Bazalgette

Dr Cary Bazalgette worked at the British Film Institute from 1979 to 2007, having previously been a teacher of English and filmmaking in London secondary schools. She has written and edited several classroom resources for media education and has published and spoken on this topic across the UK and around the world. She was Head of BFI Education from 1999–2006, leading the BFI's commitment to developing new approaches to teaching and learning about the moving image media, particularly for the 3–14 age group, and gaining a higher profile for this area of education at national policy level. Following 18 months as the BFI's Education Policy Adviser and as General Secretary of the 8-nation Steering Group for the European Charter for Media Literacy, she worked as a freelance researcher, writer and consultant specializing in media literacy and in children's media, and chaired the Media Education Association for two years. In 2018 she completed a PhD at the Institute of Education, London, on 2 year olds' encounters with moving-image media; her book *How Toddlers Learn the Secret Language of Movies* was published by Palgrave Macmillan in 2022. She lives in North London, has two children and three grandchildren.

Dr Marcel Broersma

Marcel Broersma is Professor of Media and Journalism Studies at the University of Groningen, The Netherlands. He is the director of the Centre for Media and Journalism Studies and its Digital Inclusion Lab. His research focuses on digital literacy and inclusion, media use and digital journalism on which he published widely. He is currently directing the research project "Informed Citizenship for All. Digital Literacy as a Prerequisite for an Inclusive Society", funded by the Dutch Research Council, SKSG, the National Library of the Netherlands and the Dutch Ministry of the Interior, and he is the chairperson of the Digital Literacy Coalition.

Dr Noel Brown

Dr Noel Brown is Senior Lecturer in Film at Liverpool Hope University. He has written several books on aspects of children's film, family entertainment and animation, including *Contemporary Hollywood Animation* (Edinburgh University Press, 2021), *The Children's Film: Genre, Nation and Narrative* (Columbia University Press, 2017), *British Children's Cinema: From The Thief of Bagdad to Wallace and Gromit* (I.B. Tauris, 2016), and *The Hollywood Family Film: A History, from Shirley Temple to Harry Potter* (I.B. Tauris, 2012). He is also co-editor of *Toy Story: How Pixar Reinvented the Animated Feature* (Bloomsbury, 2018) and *Family Films in Global Cinema: The World Beyond Disney* (I.B. Tauris, 2015), and editor of *The Oxford Handbook of Children's Film* (Oxford University Press, 2022). He is editor of the 'Children's Film and Television' series, published by Edinburgh University Press, and is currently working on a volume examining radical children's film and television as part of the series.

Vanessa Chapman

Internationally respected award-winning media executive Vanessa Chapman has an extensive network of contacts and proven experience in content and business strategy, organisational and management structures, fundraising and investment. She is director of a number of businesses, including VJC Media, her own creative and business agency that works with broadcasters, media companies, brands and investors. Previously, Vanessa was Controller of Children's & Family Programmes for ITV and MD of The LEGO Company's international media division.

Greg Childs OBE

Greg worked for over 25 years at the BBC, mainly as a director, producer and executive producer of children's programmes. He created the first Children's BBC websites and, as Head of Children's Digital, developed and launched the children's channels, CBBC and CBeebies. Greg left the BBC in 2004 and went on to advise producers on digital, interactive and cross-platform strategies, and broadcasters on channel launches, digital futures and operational management. He was in the launch teams for Teachers TV and the CITV Channel in the UK, and was advisor to the Al Jazeera Children's Channel for three years. He also consulted with the European Broadcasting Union on their Children's and Youth strategy. As Editorial Director of the Children's Media Conference, Greg has grown this annual event into a gathering of 1,200+ delegates, with over 200 speakers, and spin-off events and activities year-round. At the same time he spent 15 years as one of the Heads of Study for the German Akademie für Kindermedien.

Greg was awarded an OBE in the 2022 New Year Honours List.

Nigel Clarke

A hugely recognisable face (and voice) in presenting and hosting, Nigel Clarke is a vastly experienced and versatile performer across entertainment, dance and music. Nigel is well known for CBeebies *The Baby Club* and *The Toddler Club* and has been involved with countless TV and live shows across multiple channels and networks.

A proud father of three himself, in 2020 Nigel also founded the British Podcast Awards nominated *Dadvengers*. With over nearly half a million listeners, it's also a website and community that features celebrity guests and is an incredible parenting network to support fathers with resources, info and sharing intimate parenting experiences.

Geoff Coward

Geoff is a BAFTA and RTS award winning television director with a wide range of credits in multi-camera OB/Studio and single camera productions.

He started his directing career in live news for CNN, ITN and the BBC where he directed the launch of BBC News 24 before taking the reins at *Breakfast With Frost*. He now specialises in children's content, with credits including *Swashbuckle*, *Mr Tumble*, *Art Ninja*, *Gigglebiz* and *The Makery*, as well as the ever popular Christmas Panto and Shakespeare performances for CBeebies. Geoff is also Creative Director for Playa Digital, an indie specialising in producing children's content for streaming platforms.

Dr Eleanor Dare

Dr Eleanor Dare is a Senior Teaching Associate and organising member of the Arts Creativities Research group at the University of Cambridge. Eleanor has served as a digital specialist for the Pathways Digital project at the Faculty of Education as well as an executive editor for the Cambridge Journal of Education. Eleanor is also a part time Lecturer in Practice Based Research and Media specialising in Games. Formerly Reader in Digital Media at the RCA and Head of Programme for MA Digital Direction, Eleanor is a peer reviewer for the AHRC and EPSRC as well as a board member for the Theatre in the Mill Bradford. Eleanor has exhibited many installations and VR works nationally and internationally.

Dr Amy Davis

Dr Amy M. Davis is a lecturer in Film Studies at the University of Hull whose specialization is Disney (classical Disney animation history in particular). She is the author of multiple papers, including "The Dark

Prince and Dream Women: Walt Disney and Mid-Twentieth Century American Feminism" (Historical Journal of Film, Radio, and Television, 2005) as well as the books *Good Girls & Wicked Witches: Women in Disney's Feature Animation* (2006), *Handsome Heroes & Vile Villains: Men in Disney's Feature Animation* (2013), and editor of *Discussing Disney* (2019), all published by John Libbey & Co./University of Indiana Press. Any remaining space in her work brain not devoted to Disney is focused on ghosts and writing modern Gothic literature.

Camilla Deakin

Camilla Deakin is an award-winning creative producer with a career in film and TV spanning over 30 years. In 2002 Camilla and her colleague Ruth Fielding founded Lupus Films which has grown to become one of the UK's leading animation studios, specialising in high-quality family entertainment and adaptations of much-loved classic book properties. Lupus Films productions include BAFTA nominated specials *The Snowman* and *The Snowdog*, *We're Going on a Bear Hunt*, and International Emmy Kids winner *The Tiger Who Came to Tea*, as well as animated feature films such as the award-winning *Ethel & Ernest* and the forthcoming *Kensuke's Kingdom*, currently selected in competition at Annecy Film Festival.

Jackie Edwards

Jackie is a passionate advocate for public service television and until very recently, was living her dream job as the Head of the British Film Institute's Young Audiences Content Fund, responsible for the implementation of this game-changing UK Government initiative to stimulate the provision of public service content for audiences of 0–18.

This hugely successful three-year pilot awarded £44.1M of funding supporting 61 brand new commissions for UK children and teens and funded the development of a further 160 new projects, over 9% of which have already been commissioned. Shows supported range from *Milo* and *The World According to Grandpa* through to *Big Boys* and *Don't Hug Me I'm Scared*.

The Fund has been a powerful lever in stimulating a sector in market failure. Jackie joined the BFI in 2019 from BBC Children's where she was the Head of Acquisitions and Independent Animation, responsible for pre-buying and acquiring live-action and animated programming for CBeebies, CBBC and iPlayer. She joined the BBC in 2008 as Content Manager and Executive Producer.

Jackie worked on a wide range of programming including *Rastamouse*, *Hey Duggee*, *Octonauts*, *Boy Girl Dog Cat Mouse Cheese*, *Clangers*, *Poppies* and *The Next Step*.

Prior to the BBC Jackie was an award-winning producer in the independent sector for 14 years, developing, financing and producing specials and series for young audiences.

Joe Godwin

Joe joined BBC Children's as a trainee in 1989, becoming an assistant producer, studio director and producer on shows such as *Record Breakers*, *Going Live* and *Blue Peter*. In 1997 he became Editor of Children's Presentation before joining Nickelodeon in 2000, where he had a number of jobs including Head of Original Production and Interactive Director.

Joe returned to the BBC in 2005 as Head of Children's Entertainment, then Head of News, Factual and Entertainment. In 2009 he was appointed as Director BBC Children's, responsible for all of the BBC's services for children. He led the department's move from London to Salford in 2011.

In 2015 Joe left the world of children's media after 25 years to become Director BBC Midlands and the BBC Academy. In 2020 he took up the role of Director of Partnerships for BBC Nations & Regions, responsible for key partnerships across the UK – including the Commonwealth Games and UK City of Culture. In 2021, he retired and developed a new partnership with a Whippet called Dylan.

As well as being a founder patron and board member of the Children's Media Foundation, Joe is a trustee of Action for Children's Arts.

Prof Usha Goswami

Usha Goswami CBE FRS FBA is Professor of Cognitive Developmental Neuroscience at the University of Cambridge and a Fellow of St John's College, Cambridge. She is also founding Director of the Centre for Neuroscience in Education. After training as a primary school teacher, Usha decided to pursue research in child psychology. Her core interests are the neural mechanisms underpinning language acquisition, including relationships to the rhythmic structure of infant- and child-directed speech and the brain basis of dyslexia and speech and language difficulties. She is researching the potential utility of assistive listening technology, coupled with music- and rhythm-based behavioural interventions.

Dr Matt Hills

Matt Hills is Professor of Fandom Studies at the University of Huddersfield. He has published widely on both *Doctor Who* and media fandom. Forthcoming publications include the co-edited *Adventures Across Space and Time: A Doctor Who Reader* for Bloomsbury, and the sole-authored *Fan Studies* for Routledge. Tom Baker remains his favourite Doctor.

Anna Home OBE

Anna is Chair of the CMF Board and a Founder Patron of the organisation. Anna joined BBC radio in 1960 and started in Children's Television in 1964 where she worked as a researcher, then Director, Producer and Executive Producer, latterly specialising in Children's Drama.

She started *Grange Hill*, the controversial school series. From 1981–86 she worked at the ITV company TVS where she was Deputy Director of Programmes. In 1986 she returned to the BBC as Head of Children's programmes responsible for all children's output. She revived the Sunday teatime classic dramas and one of her last decisions before retiring was to commission *Teletubbies*.

After retiring from the BBC, Anna was Chief Executive of The Children's Film

& Television Foundation until it merged into CMF in 2012.

Anna has won many awards including a BAFTA lifetime achievement award. She was the first chair of the BAFTA Children's Committee, has chaired both the EBU Children's and Youth Working Group and the Prix Jeunesse International Advisory Board. Anna was the Chair of the Save Kids' TV Campaign and the Showcomotion Children's Media Conference Advisory Committee. She now Chairs the Board of the Children's Media Conference, and is a Board member of Screen South.

Rebekkah Hughes

Rebekkah is Design Manager for Oriel Square, a strategy, research and publishing specialist focused on education. Rebekkah oversees the creative side of Oriel Square's design projects, including resource management, commissioning artwork, illustrators and designers, as well as fulfilling internal design needs. This is the second time she has designed the *Children's Media Yearbook*.

Estelle Hughes

Estelle Hughes joined Sky Kids in late 2019 as a Commissioning Editor. Previously she was an independent Executive Producer of *Thunderbirds Are Go* for ITV Studios and joint owner of 3Line Media who produced *Driver Dan's Story Train*.

Prior to independent production Hughes was Controller at CITV working on shows including *Ministry of Mayhem*, *Pocoyo* and *My Life As A Popat*. Earlier roles include Deputy Head of Acquisitions and Animation at CBBC and Head of Development at Disney Channel UK.

Nigel Humberstone

Nigel Humberstone is a film music composer and founding member of In The Nursery, the Sheffield-based band who have released more than 30 albums since 1981 with music featured in numerous film soundtracks and theatrical trailers.

Parallel to their studio works, In The Nursery have developed their Optical Music Series, an ongoing repertoire of new soundtracks for silent films.

Emma Hyman

Emma Hyman is the Creative Director of Tiny House Productions, a boutique production company specialising in high quality content for children and families. With 20 years TV experience, mostly developing entertainment and factual entertainment for adults at a variety of production companies, Emma decided to follow her heart and specialise in what she loves most, creating shows for kids and their families. Since setting up Tiny House Productions, Emma has created CBeebies hits *The Baby Club* and *The Toddler Club* and the immersive gameshow *Don't Unleash The Beast* for CITV as well as several kids and family podcasts.

Sharna Jackson

Sharna Jackson is an author and curator who creates work to encourage children and young people to participate in arts, culture and publishing. Her debut novel *High Rise Mystery* (2019) was awarded the Waterstones Children's Book Prize, Young Readers in 2020.

Her latest novel, *The Good Turn* (2022) is set in her hometown, Luton. She is currently writing a video game with Die Gute Fabrik.

As a curator she has worked for and at institutions including Tate, Site Gallery, Design Museum, The Broad and London Games Festival where she curates an annual show, *Ensemble*.

Kyle Jenkins

Kyle Jenkins is the Acquisitions and Programme Director at Milkshake! Channel 5 and oversees all editorial elements of the content pipeline from pitch submission to programme delivery, including the development and production of original commissions, acquisitions and short form as a Commissioning Executive. Kyle is currently working across a wide slate of exciting new programmes as

Executive Producer for the preschool audience including *Tweedy & Fluff*, *Pip & Posy*, *Milo*, *Cooking With The Gills* and *Show Me How*. Kyle has worked in children's TV for over 10 years, starting in production and development at Nickelodeon, before moving into production management and producing shows including *Tickety Toc* and *Floogals* for Nickelodeon, Milkshake!, Universal Kids at Zodiak Kids Studios and Nevision Studios 1 Productions. Kyle also produces conference sessions for the Children's Media Conference and sits on the Advisory Committee.

Dr Pia Jensen

Pia Majbritt Jensen is Associate Professor at the Department of Media Studies and Journalism and Director of the Centre for Transnational Media Research at Aarhus University, Denmark. An audience, industry and production scholar, projects include an EU Horizon2020 project on European crime narratives and an Independent Research Fund Denmark project on the production and reception of audiovisual fiction for children. She has published widely and co-edited *New Patterns in Global TV Formats* (2016), *The Global Audiences of Danish TV Drama* (2020), *Danish TV Drama: Global lessons from a small nation* (2020), and the forthcoming *Audiovisual content for children and adolescents in The Nordics* (2023).

Hannie Kirkham

Hannie Kirkham is Research and Strategy Manager for Oriel Square, a strategy, research and publishing specialist focused on education. Hannie leads strategy, market research and product development alongside thought leadership publications and events, and customer insights projects. She has over ten years experience in educational publishing for print and digital media in the UK and internationally, and is a primary school governor. Hannie also has an interest in the intersection between children's education and entertainment and has worked with the Children's Media Conference as Newsletter Editor, Blogger and Producer. This is her second Co-Editorship for the *Children's Media Yearbook*.

David Kleeman

Strategist, analyst, author, speaker, once and future traveler, connector – David Kleeman has led the children's media industry in developing sustainable, child-friendly practices for 35+ years.
As SVP of Global Trends for strategy/research consultancy and digital studio Dubit, David is passionate about kids' evolving possibilities for entertainment, engagement, play and learning, while recognising that child development remains constant.

David is advisory board chair to the international children's TV festival Prix Jeunesse, and on the Children's Media Association board and the Facebook Youth Advisory Board.

Terri Langan

Terri is head of children's for Hello Halo Kids in Glasgow. As well as creating and developing children's content, she is also executive producer for all productions including nature and wildlife series *Ranger Hamza's Eco Quest*; scripted live action / animation hybrid *Dog Squad* and science gameshow *Get Set Galactic*. As well the day job, she has also designed training courses for ScreenSkills and is a member of the Children's TV Skills Council.

Johnny Leagas

Johnny Leagas is an Executive Producer and children's audio creator who has been at the heart of UK Children's audio content for over 15 years. He headed the BBC Children's audio team and was responsible for CBeebies Radio and young people's audio content. Then moving to take up the role of Audio Lead for tonies, an exciting children's audio platform, responsible for creating original and licenced content productions for the UK & Irish market. Johnny is now a successful freelance consultant, executive producer and content creator, specialising in children's audio content development and production.

johnleagas@gmail.com

Prof Sonia Livingstone

Prof Sonia Livingstone DPhil (Oxon), FBA, FBPS, FAcSS, FRSA, OBE is a Professor in the Department of Media and Communications at the London School of Economics and Political Science.

She is the author of 20 books on children's online opportunities and risks, including *Parenting for a Digital Future: How Hopes and Fears about Technology Shape Children's Lives*. Sonia has advised the UK government, European Commission, European Parliament, Council of Europe and other national and international organisations on children's rights, risks and safety in the digital age.

Dr Anastasiya Lopukhina

Dr Anastasiya Lopukhina is a Postdoctoral Research Fellow at Royal Holloway, University of London. She's an expert on the use of eye-tracking to make inferences about cognitive processing in infants, children, and adults. She's studied typical and atypical child populations including children with dyslexia, developmental language disorder, and Down's syndrome.

Gráinne Mc Guinness

An award winning creator of standout stories for young children that encourage them to see the world in different ways, Gráinne is Creative Director at Paper Owl Films, growing ambitious content for international audiences.

Creator of *Pablo* (CBeebies, RTÉJr. and CAKE) and *Happy the Hoglet* (CITV, RTÉJr. & Aardman)
Gráinne is leading an exciting development slate which includes *Pablo: Boy Meets School* (BBC, RTÉJr. & CAKE), *Bock-Bock Chicken* (CAKE), *Lí Ban* (Aardman), *Mr. Dog* (Jetpack Distribution) and *Finding Audrey* (Sinking Ship Entertainment).

Denise Mensonides

Denise Mensonides is a PhD student at the Centre for Media and Journalism Studies at the University of Groningen. In her project 'Digital Literacy in the Context of the Family' she explores how children (8–12) from differing socioeconomic backgrounds develop digital literacy. Within this project she focusses on issues surrounding digital citizenship and news literacy, digital resilience, and the development of social capital. Her project is part of the broader research project "Informed Citizenship for All. Digital Literacy as a Prerequisite for an Inclusive Society", funded by the Dutch Research Council, SKSG, the National Library of the Netherlands and the Dutch Ministry of the Interior. Denise has a background in Law as well as a MSc in Pedagogical Sciences from the University of Groningen.

Jamila Metran

Jamila is an International Aquisitions and Children's Media Consultant who previously headed up Sony Networks' portfolio of kids channels at Sony Pictures Entertainment. Overseeing scheduling, strategy and programme acquisitions, Jamila was responsible for all three UK channels, as well as Pop Africa and the recently launched Pop Italy. Previously channel head at CITV, Jamila was part of the team that launched the CITV channel in March 2006. During her time there she was instrumental in bringing big brands to the channel that continue to be the backbone of CITV today, including the LEGO franchise, *Mr Bean: The Animated Series*, and *Horrid Henry*, and was responsible for negotiating the successful partnership between CITV and Warner Bros/Turner Broadcasting. Her commissions while at CITV include, among many, the first ever kids version of *Fort Boyard*, *Thunderbirds Are Go!*, *Robozuna*, *Scrambled* and *Bear Grylls Survival School*. Jamila began her career in distribution, holding roles at Portman Film and TV and Fireworks International.

Dr Ana Oliveira

Dr Ana Filipa Oliveira is an assistant professor at Lusófona University and an integrated researcher at the Centre for Research in Applied Communication, Culture, and New Technologies (CICANT). She holds a PhD in Communication Studies. She has a Bachelor's degree in Communication Sciences: Journalism and a Master's in Marketing. She is engaged in various

European and national research projects related to media literacy, youth, and citizenship. She collaborates with several NGOs, institutions, and informal groups promoting educational activities for young people focused on citizenship, society, media, and creativity. Since 2022 she is a vice-chair for ECREA's Children, Youth and Media section.

ana.filipa.oliveira@ulusofona.pt

Marc Ollington

Marc held leadership roles at 21st Century Fox, for over a decade. Joining the organisation in 1998, and working across global TV brands including FX and FOX Sports. He led the marketing strategy and creative for award-winning TV shows including *The Walking Dead*, *The X-Files* and the Oscar winner *Free Solo*. He also was responsible for European brand strategy for National Geographic and launched the Bundesliga on FOX Sports. After leaving 21CF Marc took up a role at Sky, as their Entertainment Marketing Director, and was accountable for launching hits including *Roald and Beatrix*, *I Hate Suzie* and *The Undoing*.

Having successfully consulted for the BAFTA award winning Magic Light Pictures, formulating and executing their marketing strategy, he took up a full time position with them in April 2021 as their Marketing Director.

In his spare time, Marc has been a local radio DJ, managed a Glastonbury headlining 1990s indie rock group and co-written a book about Arsenal FC.

Dr Becky Parry

Dr Becky Parry is author of *Children, Film and Literacy* and was previously inaugural director for the Showcomotion children's film festival in Sheffield. Becky specialises in research focused on children's film and film education. Her doctoral research won the UKLA Research Award and insights from this research are published in animated form. Becky is currently working on creative learning projects with Chol Arts and Children's Capital of Culture. She is proud to be a board member for the

European Children's Film Association (ECFA) and excited to be developing a new programme of work focused on the development of screen-writing for children in the UK.

Nigel Pickard

Nigel Pickard developed and produced a wide range of programmes before becoming Controller of Children's and Family at TVS in 1986. In 1998, he moved to ITV to be Controller of Children's and Youth Programmes, responsible for the commissioning and scheduling of all ITV children's output. In 2000, he was appointed Controller of BBC Children's overseeing the launch of two new channels, CBBC and CBeebies.

In 2003, Nigel was invited back to ITV as Director of Programmes, where his remit was the scheduling and commissioning of the entire ITV output including all drama, entertainment, comedy, factual and religious programmes as well as the acquisition of all films and content from abroad.

After three successful years overseeing major commissions such as *The X Factor*, *Britain's Got Talent* and *Dancing on Ice*, he joined RDF as Group Director of Kids, Family Entertainment and Drama, where, amongst others, he has been responsible for commissions such as *Mister Maker*, *Dani's House*, *Escape from Scorpion Island* and *Tickety Toc* as well as the CBeebies landmark series, *Waybuloo*. After the merger with Zodiak Group in 2010, Nigel assumed the role of CEO MEAA, Zodiak UK Kids.

Nigel is Creative Director, Kids and Family at Nevision. He was a founder member of the Save Kids' TV Executive Committee and became a Board member of The Children's Media Foundation in January 2012.

Martin Pope

Martin Pope is joint CEO and co-founder of Magic Light Pictures, one of the UK's leading entertainment companies which makes high-quality and imaginative content for audiences, families and children worldwide. Prior to forming Magic Light, Martin ran his own company and before

that spent nine years in BBC Films, starting as a runner taking Faye Dunaway her lunch, and finishing with producing roles on films from directors including John Madden and John Schlesinger. Previous feature productions include Magic Light's *Chico and Rita*, European Film Award winning and Oscar nominated animated feature; *Wild Target*; *Glorious '39*; *The Cottage*; *Touch of Pink*; *The Heart of Me*; *Lawless Heart*; as well as tv dramas such as *The Turn of the Screw* with Colin Firth. Martin is on the board of ACE Producers and is joint Vice-President.

Dr Kruakae Pothong

Dr Kruakae Pothong is a Researcher at 5Rights and visiting research fellow in the Department of Media and Communications at London School of Economics and Political Science. Her current research focuses on child-centred design of digital services. Her broader research interests span the areas of human-computer interaction, digital ethics, data protection, internet and other related policies. She specialises in designing social-technical research, using deliberative methods to elicit human values and expectations of technological advances, such as the Internet of Things (IoT) and distributed ledgers.

Prof Kathleen Rastle

Professor Kathleen Rastle is a Professor of Cognitive Psychology at Royal Holloway, University of London. She's interested in the neurocognitive processes that underpin skilled reading and learning to read. She advises governments and other organisations around the world on how to improve children's reading outcomes through application of the science of reading.

Dr Eva Redvall

Eva Novrup Redvall is Associate Professor and Head of the Section for Film Studies and Creative Media Industries at the University of Copenhagen. Her research focuses on screenwriting, production and policy, currently as Principal Investigator of the Reaching Young Audiences research project. She has published widely, e.g.

the monograph *Writing and Producing Television Drama in Denmark: From The Kingdom to the Killing* and co-edited several books on transnational television, film and TV co-production and the Nordic screen industries. Besides her academic work, she is a film critic for the Danish newspaper Information and board member of The Danish Film Institute.

Michael Rose

Michael Rose is joint CEO and co-founder of Magic Light Pictures, one of the UK's leading entertainment companies which makes high-quality and imaginative content for audiences, families and children worldwide. Prior to forming Magic Light, Michael headed up the feature film division of UK studio Aardman Animations. He was executive producer of their animated features *Chicken Run* and the Oscar and BAFTA winning *Wallace & Gromit: Curse of the Wererabbit*. He also produced Nick Park's 1995 Oscar winning Wallace and Gromit film, *A Close Shave*. Before joining Aardman in 1994, Michael was a buyer at Channel Four Television. He started his career programming art house cinemas in Plymouth and Bristol.

Dr Vilde Schanke Sundet

Vilde Schanke Sundet is an Associate Professor in Media and Communication at Oslo Metropolitan University and the Project Leader of 'GLOBAL NATIVES? Serving youth on global media platforms' at the University of Oslo. The GLOBAL NATIVES project focuses on youth entertainment media. It investigates youth as a potential new media generation and the actions taken by national media and policymakers to stay relevant. Sundet has published multiple journal articles and two books, including *Television Drama in the Age of Streaming*.

Emma Scott

Emma recently established Cultivation Partners, a consultancy advising leaders who want to grow and transform their brands and businesses across broadcasting, publishing and the creative industries.

Previously Emma created Beano Studios, where she powered the Beano's transformation from an 80 year old comic to a global, International Emmy, nominated Indie, a high-growth kid's digital content platform and delivered double digit publishing growth.

Emma has driven the conception and expansion of ground-breaking TV and digital content throughout her career. Emma was Chief of Staff for the BBC Director-General and launched Freeview, the UK's first free digital TV platform. She went on to spearhead the creation of Freesat, the UK's satellite and streaming service, where she was CEO of the joint venture between the BBC and ITV.

Emma is Chair of the children's reading charity, World Book Day.

Laura Sinclair

Laura Sinclair is a Doctoral Researcher at Cardiff University's School of Journalism, Media and Culture researching gender representation on children's preschool public service broadcast television. Conducted through a multi-method approach of textual analysis and participant observation, the research focusses on better understanding children's interaction with gender on- and off-screen and how this influences children's construction of gender norms. Laura has published research that questions the current state of representation and how young people experience seeing themselves on screen. Laura is an Associate Fellow of the Higher Education Academy, Guest Lecturer and is also currently working as a Project Officer on the UKRI Strength in Places Funded research and development programme, Media Cymru.

Dr Carla Sousa

Dr Carla Sousa holds a PhD in Communication Sciences, a Master's Degree in Clinical and Health Psychology and a Bachelor's Degree in Psychology. Her main research interests are directed toward media studies, with a particular focus on games, inclusion, behaviour, learning, and human diversity. In Lusófona University (Portugal), Carla is part of the Centre for

Research in Applied Communication, Culture, and New Technologies (CICANT) and is an Assistant Professor on the Bachelor's Degrees in Psychology and Videogames. Carla has been part of several national and internationally funded projects and scientific networks. Since 2022, Carla has been an individual ambassador for the non-profit Women in Games and, since 2023, a member of the advisory board of ECREA.

carla.patricia.sousa@ulusofona.pt

Prof Martin Spinelli

Martin Spinelli is Professor of Podcasting and Creative Media at the University of Sussex and one quarter of the children's media and mental health company Rezilience Ltd. He is Executive Producer on the Webby and ARIA award-winning podcast *The Rez*, and his other benchmark productions are archived in the Museum of Television & Radio, and in the Martin Spinelli Collection of the Poetry and Rare Books Archive at the University at Buffalo.

He is founding editor of the *Bloomsbury Podcast Studies* book series and has authored with Lance Dann the foundational text in the field, *Podcasting: The Audio Media Revolution*.

Dr Sonia Tiwari

Dr Sonia Tiwari is a researcher at Penn State University in the College of Education, where she develops child-focused learning experiences involving design of toys, games, picture books, AR experiences and other emerging media. She has a background in character design and animation in the gaming industry. Her current research explores the design and development of kid-friendly virtual influencers, ethical co-creation with generative AI for children's media, and encouraging maker culture through the design of sustainable toys.

Simon Tomkins

Simon manages the programming and scheduling of ITV's youngest-skewing channels, ITV2; ITVBe, and CITV. He strategically plans the direction of the channels working across a range of youth-skewing brands including *Love Island* and *Celebrity Juice* for ITV2; *The Only Way Is Essex* and *The Real Housewives of Cheshire* for ITVBe, and *Scrambled* and *Spy School* for CITV. He also manages littleBe, the recently launched preschool zone on ITVBe. Simon's previous roles at ITV include Head of Scheduling for a number of channels including ITV2, ITV3, and ITV4.

Stavros Triseliotis

As a Head Industry Analyst at The Insights Family, Stavros has a sharp grasp of the macro and regional trends that impact industries catering to kids and families. With a strong professional and academic background in business and marketing, he brings a strategic perspective to his work. Since 2019, Stavros has been researching the attitudes and behaviours of young audiences. He believes that insight into kids' minds is the key to not only reaching the wider family, but also preparing for the future.

Dr Anna van Cauwenberge

Anna van Cauwenberge is an Associate Research Director in Ipsos' European Public Affairs Team in Belgium, where she is responsible for leading the team's communications research for European public authorities, including the European Commission and the European Parliament. Prior to this, she worked as a tenured Assistant Professor in Political Communication at the University of Groningen. Anna has about 15 years of experience in managing research projects to understand how citizens, and young people in particular, get informed about and engaged with social and political issues and organisations. She has an MA in Communication Science from Ghent University, and a PhD in Social Sciences from the KU Leuven and Radboud University Nijmegen (joint degree).

Dr Walter van Heuven

Dr Walter van Heuven is an Associate Professor of Psychology at University of Nottingham. He studies monolingual and bilingual language comprehension in children and adults, and is especially interested in how subtitles can support understanding in these groups. He has also pioneered the use of subtitles to study the language content of television and film.

Colin Ward

Colin Ward now works as a lecturer in film and television production at the University of York. He spent over 20 years working in children's TV, first as a producer and director for Citv before leaving to join the BBC, where he won a Bafta for *Raven*. He is also Deputy Director of the Children's Media Foundation.

Dr Ashley Woodfall

Dr Ashley Woodfall worked in television for many years before joining the teaching and research community at Bournemouth University (BU). He is a Fellow of the Royal Society of Arts and the Higher Education Academy. He holds an MA in producing film and television, a PGCE in educational practice and a PhD in children's media engagement, with a primary research focus on children and their media experiences/lives. He is Co-convenor of the Children's Media Foundation (CMF) Academic Advisory Board and a member of the CMF's Executive Group. He teaches undergraduate and postgraduate students media theory and production, with a particular interest in children's and cross-platform media. Ashley is a Senior Principal Academic at BU, having previously been Head of the Department of Media Production and Programme Leader of BA (Hons) Television Production.

Ashley's practice experience includes producing and directing factual, news, continuity, promos, commercials, entertainment and comedy; often with an interactive slant, and mostly within Children's TV. Whilst at Nickelodeon he devised, produced and directed innovative interactive music and game shows. For BBC he created multi-platform content that spanned online, interactive and broadcast. Ashley's career began within MTV and LWT's camera departments, and he still very much enjoys picking up a camera (video or stills) when the opportunity arrives.

Dr Dylan Yamada-Rice

Dr Dylan Yamada-Rice is a researcher and artist specialising in play and storytelling for children. Having a doctorate in Education and MA degrees in Research Methods, Early Childhood Education and Japanese Semiotics her work crosses academia and industry. She is a Co-Founder of a storytelling consultancy and studio called X||dinary Stories, as well as an Associate Professor in Immersive Storytelling at the University of Plymouth.

Her research sits at the intersection of experimental design and social sciences, focusing on digital storytelling, games and play on a range of platforms such as apps, augmented and virtual reality, as well as new content for television, all with an emphasis on media for children.

Dr David Zendle

David Zendle is the director of the Digital Observatory, a research organisation that seeks to help organisations and individuals understand changing digital ecosystems through the use of big behavioural data. David is a Lecturer in Computer Science at the University of York; an academic affiliate of the Behavioural Insights Team; and a member of the Advisory Board for Safer Gambling, the statutory body that advises the UK Gambling Commission on harm minimisation. David is an author of several key references regarding digital monetisation and is considered one of the world's leading experts on the convergence of video games and gambling.